Richard
Peirce

Cuddle Me
Kill Me

DEDICATION

*This book is dedicated to all the
lions and other large predators
bred in captivity for profit, who
were not as lucky as Obi and Oliver,
and who suffered and died
young at the hands of humans.*

Published by Struik Nature
(an imprint of Penguin Random House
South Africa (Pty) Ltd)
Reg. No. 1953/000441/07
The Estuaries, 4 Oxbow Crescent
(off Century Avenue), Century City, 7441 South Africa
PO Box 1144, Cape Town, 8000 South Africa

Visit **www.penguinrandomhouse.co.za** and join the Struik
Nature Club for updates, news, events and special offers.

First published in 2018 by Struik Nature
10 9 8 7 6 5 4 3 2 1

Publisher: Pippa Parker
Editor: Helen de Villiers
Designer: Janice Evans
Proofreader: Thea Grobbelaar

Reproduction by Hirt & Carter Cape (Pty) Ltd
Printed and bound by DJE Flexible Print Solutions

Print: 978 1 77584 593 5
ePub: 978 1 77584 594 2

AUTHOR'S NOTE

The substance of the story of Obi and Oliver told in Part One is true. However, where I don't know exactly what happened I have had to guess what could have taken place.

In the areas of public opinion, conservation and national and international laws, issues involved with the breeding of lions in captivity are continuously evolving. Since going to press it is likely that some of the facts in this book have changed and the positions and opinions of some NGOs and government departments modified. I have made every effort to accommodate this eventuality, and at the back of the book readers will find a 'Stop Press' update listing relevant developments that I became aware of between finishing the book and finally going to press.

Richard Peirce

Exploring lion tourism was a necessary part of my research.

CONTENTS

PART TWO • JOURNEY OF DISCOVERY

PART THREE • KILL ME

PART FOUR • PAST, PRESENT AND FUTURE

FOREWORD

by Chris Mercer

This book ought to be compulsory reading for all players in the tourism industry. Wildlife author Richard Peirce has done his homework. He and his photographer wife Jacqui have travelled around South Africa visiting facilities that pose as 'wildlife sanctuaries', only to find that, almost without exception, these are sordid lion farms, breeding living targets for canned lion hunting.

The lion farmers are astute and hide their cruel and squalid enterprises behind an elaborate veil of public relations. Reading their websites, one would think that they are God's answer to all the problems relating to lion conservation. Fine-sounding but meaningless mantras are scattered across the web pages: 'every tame lion hunted is a wild lion saved'; 'our tame lions will be released back to the wild'; 'we love our lions' – these are the lies that hide the cruelty and the greed.

The people at whom these self-serving claims are aimed are largely gullible, well-meaning, naive volunteers from the developed world. Seduced by slick public relations, they throw their savings at lion farms in order to be allowed to play with lion cubs. They are unaware that they are collectively contributing millions of dollars annually to canned lion hunting, and are also putting South African locals out of work. Voluntourism is necessary to support genuine sanctuaries, but it is an abomination when used to generate profits for commercial lion breeders.

This book strips away the lies, exposing the ugly truth. No potential volunteer who reads this book will visit a lion-breeding centre. Fraudulent voluntourism, supported by the South African government, can only thrive where misinformation goes unchallenged.

This book should become every volunteer's bible. Like Carmen Berdan's invaluable website 'Volunteers in Africa Beware', *Cuddle Me Kill Me* empowers volunteers. The author is to be congratulated for producing such an important resource.

CHRIS MERCER
Campaign Against Canned Hunting (CACH)

FOREWORD

by Ian Michler

The predator-breeding and canned-hunting fiasco of the last two decades has placed a dark and embarrassing cloud over South Africa's wildlife management history.

These practices alone are unacceptable, particularly in a society that prides itself on being progressive. But when greedy tourism operators join forces with breeders and hunters, using fraudulent marketing messages to sell interactive animal experiences, it is a shocking and shameful reflection on those involved. This also pertains to the authorities that continue to sanction the brutality towards lions and other wild species.

In the process, we have confused the conservation priorities and undermined the great work being done by the recognised conservation community – which, along with responsible tourism operators, has warned that predator facilities have little to no merit. Despite this, a deadly combination of ignorance, significant revenue streams and a perverted interpretation of sustainable use continue to keep the operators in business. This gives us insight into the challenges we face to end these practices.

In light of this, the appearance of *Cuddle Me Kill Me* by Richard Peirce, well-known author and conservationist, is all the more relevant and timely. Richard has authored a number of books in a similar vein, all well received for their compelling stories and powerful conservation messages. This is the latest in the set, but with the additional element of investigative endeavour that these industries necessitate.

Backed by in-depth research, Richard has done an excellent job in getting to the core of what goes on behind the high fences of so many farms and facilities. More importantly, he has humanised the story by showing clearly how volunteers and visitors get duped. History has shown over and again that enlightened attitudes overcome primitive practices and anachronistic behaviour. I am convinced that in time, predator breeding and all the associated activities will be judged as a terrible blight on our conservation and legislative record. *Cuddle Me Kill Me* will have made a significant contribution to the body of evidence.

IAN MICHLER
(*Blood Lions*) South Africa, 2017

ACKNOWLEDGEMENTS

Writing this book fulfils a promise to my wife Jacqui who, for many years, has urged me to write about captive lion breeding. I hope, in a small way, it will also carry on and augment the excellent public awareness work done by Gareth Patterson, The Cook Report, *Blood Lions*, The Campaign Against Canned Hunting, Four Paws, The Born Free Foundation, LionAid and many others. I would like to thank all those below for their help. Many of them work tirelessly on a daily basis to bring an end to this abhorrent type of 'livestock farming'.

- Drew Abrahamson
- Joy Adamson – author of *Born Free*, *Living Free* and *Forever Free*
- Makram Alamuddin
- Karl Ammann
- Colin Bell
- Werner Boing
- Born Free Foundation
- Stan Burger
- Harry Bush
- Thea Carroll
- Altie Clark
- Lizaene Cornwall
- Tom, Rosie and Lisa Dawe
- Chris de Wet
- Four Paws
- Mike Fynn
- Pippa Hankinson
- Paul Hart
- Tayla Hawkins
- Denise Headon
- Willi Jacobs
- Hildegaard Jager
- James, our undercover agent
- Jeremy (email enquirer)
- Dr Mark Jones

- André la Cock
- LionAid
- Cassandra MacDonald
- Chris Mercer – Campaign against Canned Hunting (CACH)
- Ian Michler
- Mike (email enquirer)
- Fiona Miles
- Nick Muller
- NSPCA
- Cathrine Scharning Nyquist
- Obi and Oliver
- Linda Park
- Gareth Patterson – author of *Dying to be Free* and *Cry for the Lions*
- Jacqueline Peirce
- Charlotte Peirce-Gregory
- Oliver Peirce-Gregory
- Hildegaard Pirker
- Professional Hunters' Association of South Africa (PHASA)
- Jolanda Schreuder
- South African Predator Association (SAPA)
- Will Travers OBE

- Linda Tucker – author of *Saving the White Lions*
- Ukutula
- Tharia Unwin
- Dries van Coller
- Carla van de Vyver – SAPA
- Henriet van Rhyn
- Bo and Mimi Wixted

And finally thanks to everybody at Struik Nature who once again dealt with a difficult author with patience, and did a brilliant job putting this book together – Pippa Parker, Helen de Villiers, Janice Evans and Belinda van der Merwe. I apologise to anyone I have inadvertently left out.

The king of the animal world

PREFACE

My previous books – *The Poacher's Moon, Giant Steps* and *Nicole* – are all true stories about real, existing animals. When I first heard about two rescued lions, Obi and Oliver, and went to meet them and their rescuers, I found their story to be both compelling and moving. However, I found the background to their story to be of equal interest, and I decided to investigate the whole issue of breeding lions in captivity.

In early 2016 I was invited by a friend to watch a fundraising screening of the film *Blood Lions* in Hermanus in the Western Cape. This powerful film had a profound impact on the audience, as well as on me, and it raised many questions. It was clearly a campaigning film, and a very powerful one, which set out to tell one particular side of the story, and so the conclusion it would reach was known from the outset. But was the situation all as one-sided as portrayed in the film? Was the portrayal wholly fair, true and accurate?

Why would volunteers pay to help raise captive lions, a practice that, if *Blood Lions* were true, only a little research would indicate was ethically tainted? What motivates lion breeders, and how would they seek to justify their actions? After the US government's 2016 decision to curtail the import of trophies from South Africa to America, to what extent did captive-bred lion hunting still exist? These were just a few of the many questions to which we decided to try and find answers.

During 2016 and 2017 my wife Jacqui and I, with the help of undercover volunteers, investigated big-cat breeding farms. Our journeys of discovery took several months; we drove thousands of kilometres to visit lion-breeding farms and lion tourist attractions, and interviewed people involved in all aspects of this sector.

We discovered that, even though the hunting aspect of the lion-breeding industry is probably no longer the primary financial income stream for breeders, it remains the flag bearer for the issue because it is visually shocking, and gained notoriety around the world when it was still prevalent. So-called 'responsible tourism' has to some extent taken over – cub petting, walking with lions, the use of lions for films and adverts, as well as for so-called awareness and education – but these serve only to milk the industry in another guise. And the sale of products derived from lion carcasses at least partly compensates lion breeders for the reduction in hunting, and keeps the wheels of the industry turning.

While Part One of this book focuses on the lives and destinies of two captive-bred lions, Part Two tells the personal story of our investigative journeys, documents the answers we found, and lays out what we hope is an objective view of captive predator breeding and all its spin-off activities in South Africa. In Part Three, the logistics of booking and participating in a hunt with a guaranteed outcome are unpacked; and in Part Four the tawdry uses and far-flung destinations of lion products are examined and conservation issues are raised; and the official South African Government standpoint is covered in an Appendix.

In over 30 years of campaigning for wildlife, which has now become my full-time occupation, I have encountered many disturbing and moving situations. Working in fish markets full of dead sharks felt like walking through marine graveyards; seeing rhinos and elephants with their horns and tusks hacked out, and looking around shops full of wildlife body parts being sold as souvenirs, are all experiences and images that will haunt me as long as I live. It is now time to expose the tragedy of the captive predator breeding industry.

My wife Jacqui and I drove thousands of kilometres to visit farms and lion tourist attractions, and interviewed people involved in all aspects of this sector.

LION FACTS

- Lions are the only cats that live in families (prides) and have a complex social structure.
- They are the second largest of the 'big cats'.
- The lion is known as the 'king of the jungle', but doesn't live in the jungle!
- Baby lions are most commonly called cubs but can also be known as 'whelps' or 'lionets'.
- Female lions (sisters) live together for life, and female cubs stay with the pride after reaching adulthood.
- Male lions are the only big cats to grow a mane, which makes them look more intimidating.
- Females are attracted to males with fuller, thicker manes.
- Lions once lived in Europe, Africa, Asia, the Middle East and northern India. They are now confined to Africa, apart from a small group in the Gir Forest in India.
- They have the loudest roar of any cat species; it can be heard up to 8 kilometres (5 miles) away.
- Lions are a common national symbol: Albania, Belgium, Bulgaria, England, Ethiopia, Luxembourg, the Netherlands and Singapore all use them as national symbols.
- Thirteen African states have lions in their coat of arms.
- Adult males are generally larger than females and, on average, weigh 180–200 kilograms.
- Lions and tigers are so closely related that, if shaved, it would be difficult to tell them apart.
- Males trying to take over a pride will often kill all the previous incumbent's cubs.
- Lions start mating at between three and four years old.
- The gestation period is about four months.

- Cubs weigh about 1.5 kilograms (3 pounds) at birth.
- Lionesses give birth away from the rest of the pride.
- Females are the main hunters and commonly hunt co-operatively.
- Grassland antelopes and zebras are common prey, but buffalo and even elephant are sometimes taken by lions.
- There can be as many as 40 lions in a pride but, more usually, three males and about 12 females.
- They can run up to 64 kilometres per hour (40 miles per hour) for short distances, and can leap over 9 (horizontal) metres (30 feet).
- Less than a century ago there were as many as 200,000 wild lions in Africa; now there are only between 20,000 and 30,000, which live in 28 range states.
- The IUCN (International Union for the Conservation of Nature) and the American Wildlife Foundation list lions as Vulnerable.
- The Latin name for lion is *Panthera leo*.
- A lion's heels don't touch the ground when it walks.
- A lion may sleep for up to 20 hours a day.

Panthera Africa

INTRODUCTION

'I have told the lions you are coming and they are waiting for you', said Cathrine as we met on the terrace of her house.

When I left, they were both staring into the wind, their manes streaming behind them.

I have always believed that animals communicate in ways we don't understand, in languages we don't speak – but that some humans can, inexplicably, communicate with them. Nevertheless, when Cathrine told me that she had spoken to the two lions, Oliver and Obi, and that they were waiting for me, I was slightly sceptical and wasn't quite sure what to expect.

Carrying my fold-up chair, I set off for the lion enclosure, and realised that while Obi was staring into the distance, completely ignoring my approach, Oliver was watching me intently from the roof of his shelter. I had not walked 15 metres before he jumped down, walked over and sat down to wait for me at the exact spot where the path would bring me to the fence.

As I walked towards him he changed from a sitting to a lying position, and yawned. He was quite relaxed; for some reason, I wasn't. Even though an electric fence separated us I was nervous, and I wondered why. Perhaps I was nervous that he wouldn't like me? To lions we are walking hamburgers, so maybe I was anxious at the proximity of an apex predator? I walked along the fence to an area shaded by a large bush, unfolded my chair and settled to watch the two lions. Oliver's extraordinary eyes followed me all the time; they are a soft, light blue, but in certain light they are nearly

16

white. He got up and walked the 20 metres along the fence, stopping opposite me, lay down again and resumed his inspection of me. Our eyes locked and I couldn't look away. As we stared steadily at one another, I wondered if Oliver would regard this staring as confrontational.

I thought his eyes looked sad but questioning, and then realised that he was engaging with me, almost 'talking', and now, writing this several weeks later, I can still remember exactly how it felt. His eyes weren't sad at all – they were soft and calm and he was saying to me 'I am your friend'. I have owned and trained dogs all my life and have often felt the same message or vibe from them, but this wasn't a labrador or a spaniel, it was a fully grown male lion.

I sat with Oliver for about an hour, and at one point had started to doze when a hornet crashed into my face. I jumped, suddenly fully awake, and looked at Oliver who was still watching me. Lions don't laugh, can't grin, and their eyes can't twinkle with amusement, but that was the vibe he gave off, so I asked him what was so funny? His answer was to get up, stalk majestically back to his shelter, jump onto the roof, and join Obi in his never-ending staring into the distance.

A few minutes later he jumped down again, padded back to me, and resumed gazing at me with his calm, friendly eyes. In due course, I packed up my chair and cameras, and walked back along the fence towards the house. Oliver matched my pace exactly as, on huge pads, he walked alongside me on his side of the fence, up until the point where the path diverted up to the house. If ever Cathrine tells me again that she has told the lions I am coming, and they are waiting for me, I won't dismiss it. I will remember this experience, which underlined for me how little we know about communication in the animal world. Ten minutes later when I drove away, Oliver had again taken up position beside Obi and they were both staring into the wind, their manes streaming behind them.

Oliver and Obi were rescued from South Africa's lion-breeding industry, where they, and thousands of others, would likely have had short lives, and become 'blood lions', either shot as trophies or for the value of their carcasses. *Cuddle Me Kill Me* is the story of Obi and Oliver. It is also the story of the thousands of other lions that were not so lucky, and had their lives cut short by human 'hunters' or other exploiters.

TERMINOLOGY

- 'Captive-bred' animals encompasses both those that are 'ranch bred' and 'tourism bred'. When used by the South African Predator Association (SAPA), 'ranch bred' indicates captive-bred lions that are reared with as little human contact as possible, whereas 'tourism-bred' lions are habituated to humans.

- 'Managed wild': These are lions on genuine reserves. They are truly wild in that they are not bred and never fed, and their only contact with humans is from visiting safari tourists and occasional veterinary intervention. However, their territory is fenced and contains a controlled population that has its freedom of movement restricted, and so the gene pool is limited. These lions are 'managed' in the sense that their genetic integrity has to be monitored. Reserve owners can apply to government for licences to shoot these lions provided they can prove they are genuinely wild and present a case for the issue of a hunting licence. They are regarded as 'wild' by the Professional Hunters' Association of South Africa (PHASA), which considers these animals suitable for hunting.

- Genuinely 'wild': In southern Africa, this applies only to lions living in areas such as Kruger, Kgalagadi, Etosha, Hwange, Tsavo, the Okavango Delta, etc., where there is no human intervention and only limited interaction (safari groups and periodic scientific studies) and the animals are free roaming.

Lions in categories 2 and 3 have the survival skills and the genetic integrity to survive in the wild, whereas the consensus among scientists, lion ecologists and genuine and knowledgeable conservationists is that captive-bred animals would not be viable in the wild, and their release could be detrimental not only to themselves but also to wild populations.

PART ONE
Cuddle me

CHAPTER 1

CAPTIVE BORN AND ORPHANED

The lioness and her cubs were shut in a small barred cage that opened onto a large enclosure surrounded by an electrified fence. Four days earlier she had given birth to three cubs, which had just finished the latest in a round-the-clock succession of feeds. The cubs slept, and she dozed.

The largest of the cubs was a light-coloured male and he slept sprawled across her throat with a tiny paw dangling near one of his mother's half-closed eyes.

The noise of an engine approaching meant little because vehicles often passed the enclosure, so the lioness took no notice of it at first. But then it stopped only a few metres from her cage, and she raised her head. The cub fell off her neck and squirmed briefly in protest before cuddling up to its sisters and going back to sleep. A man and woman dressed in khaki shorts and shirts got out of the vehicle's cab; they went to the open back and lowered the tailgate. The man leaned in and dragged out a bloody chunk of meat – part of a donkey's leg. It was obviously quite heavy because he had to swing it slowly backwards to gain the momentum that allowed him to hurl it over the fence into the lioness's enclosure. The meat hit the dry ground with a thud and threw up a small cloud of dust. The lioness was on her feet, standing in the doorway of her cage as the tempting meal landed less than 20 metres away. She knew what it was and she leapt out in one bound and was onto the meat. Behind her there was a loud clang: metal struck metal as the door of the cage crashed shut.

She had fallen for the cruellest of cruel tricks: the cubs were on one side of the bars and she was on the other. She knew what had happened; perhaps it had happened to her before. Instinct made her hang onto her meal as she ran, so she dragged the meat back to the cage gate. She then watched as the last of her three cubs was picked up by the woman and handed to the man who carried it to join the others, which were already in a small cage in the back of the pick-up truck. At only four days old, the tiny, pale-coloured male lion and his sisters still had their eyes tightly closed. The engine started and they were on their way into a life that would involve exploitation, sadness, cruelty and suffering.

The lioness's eyes were filled with a terrible anger and despair as she paced the fence and cried out for her cubs being driven away, and gradually the sound of the engine faded to nothing. The three baby lions were being taken to Cheetah Experience, a predator breeding and rearing facility in South Africa's Free State.

Thirty-year-old Lizaene Cornwall had been working as a human resources (HR) manager for a cleaning company before starting work at Cheetah Experience in 2009. When she woke up on 15 October, 2011, she was excited because she knew that three 'orphan' lion cubs were due to arrive that day. She didn't know that their arrival would be the first in a series of events that would change her life forever. A few months earlier four other orphans had arrived, but they had now grown too old for the bottle feeding and cuddling or petting that tourists pay to engage in with baby lions. The new cubs would replace the older animals as money-earning tourist magnets.

At that time, Cheetah Experience offered interactions with lion and cheetah cubs, as well as guided tours around the cages and enclosures that housed a variety of other large predators.

Volunteers came from all over the world and paid around $500 a week to help rear lion cubs that had been 'orphaned' – not by any natural event, but taken from their mother at, or soon after, birth so that they could be commercially exploited. Lizaene had worked at Cheetah Experience for two years and was paid R1,000 a month, plus her food and

Lizaene Cornwall

accommodation. She knew that her love for animals was enabling her to be exploited. But she didn't care: she was where she wanted to be, and was doing what she wanted to do. Money was neither a consideration nor a motivator.

Cheetah Experience is situated a few kilometres outside Bloemfontein off the R64. Having turned off the main tarred road, the pick-up truck had to slow down for the last couple of kilometres on the rougher graded gravel surface. The vibrations of the new road surface had woken the cubs up, and kept them awake. Towing a trail of grey dust behind it, the vehicle turned into the Cheetah Experience gate.

Oliver and his sisters were four days old when they arrived at Cheetah Experience.

Lizaene had gone about her morning's work but for the last hour had been listening for the arrival of the cubs. She knew they were very young, had only just been orphaned, and if they were not to join the 25 per cent of cubs that didn't survive, they would require continuous care and attention.

To the uninitiated, hand rearing cubs by bottle feeding looks fun and easy. Lizaene was experienced and knew that while it was often fun, it was rarely easy. It was a 24-hour-a-day, seven-days-a-week commitment full of challenges for her and dangers for the cubs.

CHAPTER 2

SURROGATE MOTHERS

At birth the cubs had each weighed just over a kilogram. With mother's milk on tap, they had all put on weight, and by the time they arrived at Cheetah Experience four days later, the male was the largest, weighing 1.5 kilograms.

Back at the breeding farm the lioness still paced the fence and cried out for her cubs, but by the time the cubs arrived at Cheetah Experience they weren't so much missing their mother as missing a good feed.

First Lizaene put them into a small den; then, together with two helpers, she prepared their first 'formula' feed. In one way, the cubs had been lucky: they had had four days of their mother's milk, and so had received a good supply of colostrum, which is also known as 'beestings' or 'first milk', and is produced by mammals for a few days after giving birth. Colostrum contains antibodies that boost the immune system; it helps the workings of the digestive tract, and it has a mild laxative effect to assist the passing of the first faecal matter called meconium. Even though the cubs had benefited from four days of mother's milk, Lizaene took no chances and made sure the milk formula contained a colostrum substitute.

Although a product was available that is close to a lioness's milk in terms of protein, fat, carbohydrate and dry-matter content, it had been

Panthera Africa

Panthera Africa

Cubs are often taken away from their mothers when only a few hours old.

Obi, shortly after his arrival at Cheetah Experience

found at Cheetah Experience that lion cubs did much better on a product designed for dogs. The cubs would be fed every 2–4 hours around the clock, which effectively meant that Lizaene and her colleagues had to set up a 24-hour milk-feeding production line.

The first feed proved to be a particular trial. After the cubs had been weighed, Lizaene and her team each picked one up in their left hand and, with a bottle in their right, started the process. The milk was warm, the nipples had been tested, the handlers were all trained and the cubs were hungry. The basics all seemed to be in place for a successful first feed, but it didn't quite work out that way. Each cub had its own idea of how to go about bottle feeding, and these ideas had nothing to do with how the handlers thought things should work! There was lots of squirming and wriggling; mouths would snap shut when a teat was offered, and then had to be gently prised open; hind legs seemed to have minds of their own, and moved in ways that didn't help. Skill, patience and humour eventually won the day and all three cubs successfully drank a few millilitres – although it was impossible to tell exactly how much had actually been consumed, because more milk had been spilt than had been drunk.

From the very first feed, Lizaene would keep a detailed record of the cubs' progress: amounts fed, weight gained, urination, defecation and any other relevant observations would all be noted. Each feed got a little easier and by the end of the fourth day all the cubs were regularly consuming 10 millilitres at each feed.

By now the cubs had been named. Because they had been born in October, it was decided to start all their names with the letter 'O'. The male became Oliver, and his two sisters Omega and Orva. Oliver drank the most and his eyes had now opened. In the next few days Orva and Omega would also open their eyes. Lizaene was beginning to relax: the cubs were feeding well, there were no complications, and for their age they were all at the correct average weight.

Before dawn on 26 October, about 50 kilometres away from Bloemfontein, and at the same farm that had bred Oliver and his sisters, the same sick drama as before was taking place, but this time one that would result in heartache for Lizaene and her volunteers over the course of the next month. Watched by keepers, a lioness had given birth to three cubs: two males and a female. Two hours later, when the keepers were sure there would be no more cubs born, they approached the cage and frightened the lioness, who ran to the far side of the enclosure, temporarily deserting her newborn cubs. Normally, she would have picked up a cub before running for safety, but so great was her fear and panic that she didn't do this.

The keepers were ready: as soon as she moved away they opened the gate and two of them went into the den and grabbed the cubs, while the third keeper kept a close eye on the lioness. They then stole away into the dawn, while an anguished and highly distressed mother paced the fence, calling out for her young. Throughout the day she returned repeatedly to the den and sniffed the place where her cubs had been born only a few hours earlier.

Lizaene was ready for the second litter of new arrivals and although she had not been told exactly how old they were, she expected a replay of the arrival of Oliver and his sisters. She would supervise the rearing of both litters, but until she was sure that neither litter had any transmissible health problems, she would be 'hands on' with only one set of cubs – Oliver and his sisters, who were used to her – while watching over the volunteers who would take on the actual handling of the new arrivals.

A white car arrived just after 10h00. A large cardboard box was handed over. It felt light and there was little movement inside. The reason for the lightness and the lack of movement became evident as soon as the box was opened: clearly, the cubs inside it were only a few hours old! Their mother had not even had time to clean them before they were snatched away, so remnants of their umbilical cords were still attached, and the cubs were still damp.

Oliver and his sisters at four days old had been robust compared to these pathetic little creatures, which presented a totally different challenge; Lizaene wondered if she would be able to pull them all through. Now she was supervising six little lives, and three of them were at extreme risk. She was used to taking responsibility, but it had never felt as heavy as this before.

CHAPTER 3
BATTLE FOR SURVIVAL

When Lizaene had first come to work at Cheetah Experience she had accepted the explanations given to her as to how cubs became orphans. She had variously been told they were abandoned, were a first-time litter and the lioness had not known what to do, had been rejected at birth, were at risk of being killed by a male, and so on. She had no reason to doubt these explanations.

Many years before, in 1997, Britain's ITV had broadcast a programme called *Making a Killing*, which exposed the highly contentious practice known as 'canned hunting' – the shooting of animals that are fenced in and unable to escape the 'hunter'. This was part of an investigative TV series called The Cook Report presented by Roger Cook. The initial impact of the programme was huge, and canned hunting was widely condemned. However, once the furore had died down things went back to normal and hunting of captive-bred lions not only continued, it expanded.

Lizaene was 16 at the time *Making a Killing* was broadcast, and was unaware of it. She went to university where she did a degree in psychology, then worked in human resources at a large cleaning company before joining Cheetah Experience as a member of staff.

In 1997 Britain's ITV channel broadcast a Cook Report episode called Making a Killing. *This was the first large-scale exposé of canned hunting.*

Investigator Roger Cook pictured with a lion.

She soon realised the orphan cubs were being used to make money. But raising cubs also cost money: they needed veterinary attention, feeding and had to be cared for, etc., so she accepted that funds had to be generated. Cubs made money by attracting volunteers who paid to raise them, and day visitors who paid to cuddle them. Later, they would be trained to walk with paying humans, and some would appear in films and advertisements, while others would be sold to zoos and private owners all over the world.

Lizaene and other staff workers and volunteers all over southern Africa constituted a large army of people who were so focused on a demanding and time-consuming job that only rarely did any of them question what they were involved in. This enabled the breeders to exploit their workers just as they were exploiting the animals they were breeding.

Eventually, all staff would become aware of the way the industry worked: that at virtually every stage of the animals' lives they were being used to generate money for breeders and other exploiters, and that the cubs the volunteers helped raise would die young from hunters' bullets. At this point, many would move on in disgust. But there was always a ready supply of others eager to take their places – until the truth dawned on them too.

The cubs newly arrived at Cheetah Experience had also been born in October so the use of an initial 'O' for their names was continued: the males became Obi and Orion, and their sister Opal.

When introducing the earlier litter to their first bottle feed, Lizaene and her helpers had been dealing with three strong, squirming and wriggling little fur-covered 'tadpoles'. The new arrivals were smaller and weaker, and Lizaene knew that their will to live would be a major factor in deciding whether or not they survived. What's more, Oliver and his sisters had had four days of their mother's milk and antibody-rich colostrum. In contrast, the three new cubs had not fed from their mother at all, which meant that not only did they lack the colostrum that was so vital for their immune systems, but they were by now also dehydrated. The staff cleaned the cubs, made sure they were warm, and an hour after they had arrived tried to get them to bottle feed. Obi took a few millilitres on the second attempt, but the other two didn't take any milk until early that evening. Lizaene's helpers tried to feed the cubs every hour to alleviate their dehydration, ensure that they got colostrum, and to build their strength. They were up all night and dozed in chairs between feeds. To add to the workload, every five or six hours Oliver and his sisters also had to be fed, cleaned and put back to sleep.

By dawn, the new cubs were a day old and all three were drinking but Lizaene didn't think it was enough, and she was especially worried about the two that hadn't fed initially. Another worry was her ability, and that of her helpers, to carry on with this punishing schedule. There were now six cubs to feed, and while the older ones were only fed five or six times a day, the others needed feeding at every opportunity. She worked out a rota for two teams for the next four days. It didn't involve much sleep but she hoped it would enable them all to carry on until the tiny cubs were feeding properly and out of immediate danger. Then they could return to some sort of normality.

Days and nights merged into a long, almost timeless existence in which the needs of the cubs dictated everything. By the end of the fourth day after the arrival of the second litter, Lizaene was much more optimistic about the new cubs' survival. They had passed meconium, were being fed at roughly the same times as Oliver and his sisters, and the amount they were drinking was increasing steadily.

A new rota was now worked out, allowing the surrogate mothers – who had begun to feel like zombies working on autopilot – to get more of the sleep they desperately needed. Mistakes happen when you are as tired as this, so getting back to a semblance of normality was both a relief and a necessity.

Oliver and his sisters were now two weeks old, had their eyes open, and were cuddly and more fun with each passing day. Cub cuddling and handling is called 'petting' in South Africa, and while some places allow the public on day visits to bottle feed cubs, this did not happen at Cheetah Experience, at least for newborn cubs. Only Lizaene and the resident volunteers would feed the cubs until they were about 10 weeks old; then the paying public would start to get their hands on them.

The younger litter was not as strong as Oliver and his sisters, nor were they developing as fast, but they seemed to be making steady progress. Then suddenly, after nine days, disaster struck. All the cubs had had mild diarrhoea but Orion got worse and two days later so did Opal. Obi remained the strongest and had milder symptoms than his siblings. The battle to save their lives meant that days again merged into nights as the team fought to replace the fluid that was continually being lost. These were desperate times for the support team: they tried their best and never gave up hope, but deep in their hearts they knew they were not going to win. In addition to the diarrhoea, the cubs had now started having fits – which looked like epilepsy – and two days later, within three hours of each other, Orion and Opal both died.

Soon after the cubs' arrival, Lizaene had noticed that Opal had a swollen front paw as if she had stepped on a bee and been stung. X-rays were taken that revealed she was missing her wrist bones and had other bone deformities. Lizaene was fairly sure the cubs had died as a result of their bad start in life – from factors such as the stress of being taken away from their mother, not fed for several hours and missing out on colostrum from mother's milk. She felt that, additionally, Opal's bone deformities were probably due to inbreeding, and there had possibly been other deformities in her organs that the X-rays had not revealed. Although the two cubs had appeared to be progressing, perhaps all the time their underlying problems had been waiting in ambush. They were both casualties of the lion-breeding industry.

There were no tears as Lizaene buried the two small, lifeless bodies side by side. Instead there was a firm set to her jaw, and in her heart a white-hot anger. This was another milestone along her journey, which would eventually lead her to condemn captive lion breeding and to work actively against it.

Obi was weak but still alive and still feeding. Lizaene was determined not to lose him and intensified her efforts, including adding finely minced chicken to the milk. She would have liked to put him in with Oliver, Orva and Omega because she was sure they would accept him, and being with other cubs would aid his recovery. However, she couldn't risk this yet in case he had some contagious infection that he might pass on.

By early December, Oliver and his sisters were nearly two months old. They were boisterous and naughty, and a couple of weeks earlier had started their introduction to solid food. Rather like the start of bottle feeding, when more milk ended up outside the cubs than inside them, feeding from bowls at first resulted in high wastage. Bowls would be stepped in, walked over and upset, but the cubs soon got the hang of it. For two weeks Obi had been kept in isolation. He was now fully over the diarrhoea, had regained all the lost weight, and was putting on more each day. He had also been introduced to solid food to bring him in line with Oliver and his sisters, in preparation for being introduced to them.

Somewhat nervously, Lizaene carried Obi towards the other three cubs and put him down. Obi was unsure, and didn't approach the others – but they approached him, led by Oliver. For the next two days, Obi lingered on the fringe of the cub pride, not yet fully part of it. There were some nasty moments but no real danger, and it was Oliver who first fully accepted him, then Omega and Orva followed their brother's lead.

Obi, Oliver, Orva and Omega had all been sired by the same father, so Obi was a half-brother to Oliver and his sisters. There was only just over a week's difference in age, but Oliver was noticeably bigger and stronger than Obi; he readily took the role of big brother and was almost protective of his smaller half-sibling. Lizaene was delighted that Obi had been accepted, and the cubs were now a strong, healthy family unit. But although it seemed they were all doing well, she never relaxed her vigilance; she was determined that no more would die.

CHAPTER 4

VOLUNTOURISM

By late December the cubs had become a visitor attraction. For a number of hours each day the public paid to cuddle them, play with them, kiss them and have photos taken with them. Playing with the cubs carried the risk of participants' getting scratched, so Lizaene and her helpers had to be alert, and often had to intercede when they saw people doing things that might lead to blood being drawn.

Oliver was clearly the leader of the little pride, Obi was slightly smaller and had a wise, grown-up air about him, while Omega and Orva were naughtier and quite enchanting. Apart from the slight size difference, it was easy to tell the half-brothers apart because they were different colours: Oliver was a very light cream, almost white, while Obi was a darker golden colour. Oliver tended to get most of the food but was assertive rather than aggressive towards his siblings. Indeed, he would sometimes give way to Obi as if he were sharing food and looking after him.

Lions are the only felines that live in family groups or prides. This means they have a social structure, a family life, and communicate in ways we sometimes understand and recognise. Anyone who has spent time with lions and watched a pride going about its daily life will have observed displays of anger, affection, tolerance, annoyance, sadness and many other familiar human emotions. Because of their family life and social hierarchy, our humanising of them is perhaps more appropriate than with other cat species.

Nothing stands still when you are working with living creatures. When Orion and Opal had died, Lizaene had been consumed by anger and sadness. The four remaining cubs were the perfect antidote to those feelings: each cub already had its own character and they could be annoying, amusing, frustrating and endearing all in the space of a few minutes. The cubs brought out strong maternal instincts in Lizaene. She looked on them as being her babies, but at the same time wished they could have been growing up with their real mothers.

The day before Christmas Eve 2011 a young Norwegian woman boarded a plane for South Africa, where she had volunteered to work for three weeks in a centre ostensibly specialising in predator-breeding conservation programmes, and rearing orphaned lion cubs. She was en route to Cheetah Experience, having already spent two weeks there earlier in the year when she had formed a strong friendship with Lizaene, and demonstrated a rare empathy with the big cats. On one occasion, shortly after being introduced to a large adolescent male lion for the first time, she was able to hug it.

After returning to Norway she had been miserable. She could not shake the feeling that she had left something precious behind, and the pull of Africa and its animals was overwhelming. She asked her boss for extra leave over Christmas and booked a three-week return trip south. When she landed in Johannesburg on Christmas Eve, the bright African summer sunshine was a welcome contrast to the grey northern European winter's day she had left behind. On the road trip from Johannesburg to Bloemfontein she breathed in the warm air, and had a strong sense of 'coming home'.

Panthera Africa

Cathrine Scharning Nyquist from Norway – initially a volunteer

Cathrine Nyquist had grown up with animals – dogs, cats and ponies were an important part of her life. As a little girl, she used to play in her grandmother's large garden and pretend she was in Africa. Her favourite place was a treehouse, and she would call out and check that there were no lions around and that it was safe before she climbed down from the tree. Years later, as an adult, after getting a degree in International Business and having started on her career, she volunteered to work with big cats. Now she was taking her dream to the next level. She looked forward to seeing Lizaene again and to new adventures and challenges.

Lions and other big cats would eventually take over Lizaene and Cathrine's lives.

Lizaene had a lot to tell her friend. They had been in regular email contact, but her irregular hours and the time difference had combined to limit opportunities to talk to each other. Cathrine had a million questions and after work that evening they started talking, carrying on into the early hours of the next day. The intense conversation was the first of many, and although the relationship quickly deepened and developed, neither of them at this stage realised where events were leading them. Each had found a vital ally, and a valued friend and partner. Lions and other big cats would eventually take over their lives permanently, and along the way they would need their friendship and partnership, and both would be tested to the limit time and time again.

CHAPTER 5

GROWING UP AS
TOURIST ATTRACTIONS

Christmas is high holiday season in South Africa and offering lion cubs for the public to cuddle and pet was a powerful tourist magnet for Cheetah Experience and similar establishments all over the country.

Oliver and his sisters were now 10 weeks old and Obi just slightly younger. They were playful, very cute, and healthy. The trauma of being removed from their mothers was in the distant past, as was the illness that had nearly killed Obi. Cheetah Experience opened every day between 10h00 and 15h00. The cubs were kept in a little enclosure and people were allowed in to play with them on an hourly basis. Cheetah Experience had many other captive predators, including tigers, servals, cheetahs, leopards and wolves, but the four lion cubs were the stars and the main reason lots of people visited.

Cathrine had now settled back into her role as a volunteer working under Lizaene. Together they supervised the interactions with the cubs and tried to ensure that they didn't get tired from too much handling, and that the visitors didn't leave with too many souvenir scratches.

The cubs' individual characters were developing: Oliver was the leader of the pride and was becoming visibly protective towards his sisters and half-brother. Omega and Orva were already little lionesses and were more active than their brothers, who slept at every opportunity. Obi often appeared distant, almost detached, and even at this young age he had a 'worldly wise' air about him. The public were unaware of these characteristics, but Lizaene and Cathrine delighted in watching from close up as their personalities developed.

Human babies are very slow in developing and for the first months of life are immobile, not doing much other than cry, feed, kick their arms and legs about, blow bubbles, make noises, and need their nappies changed. In contrast, at 10 weeks the cubs were fast on their feet, eating the food provided, were up to new tricks every day and, as long as they weren't asleep, were almost guaranteed to be doing something naughty.

Life was happy but hard; Lizaene and Cathrine got up each day at 5h30 and worked through until 22h30. They were sometimes so tired they didn't bother to eat. They were living in a bubble, and the outside world, beyond the animals, the cubs and the visitors, hardly existed. The surrogate mothers may have been exhausted when they went to bed each night, but they couldn't help looking forward to the next day,

Behind the sweet, cuddly images is a tale of exploitation and cruelty.

and the new surprises their feline 'children' would spring on them. Early on, Oliver started showing special affection for Cathrine. A strong bond grew between them and, as it strengthened, it developed a mystical, almost telepathic dimension.

Lizaene's supervisory responsibilities extended to all the animals except the cheetahs, and when she was with the lion cubs she was especially drawn to Obi, whom she found both interesting and puzzling. He was thoughtful and gentle and, although very young, had a mature, wise, almost detached air about him. When not playing or sleeping he would lie by the fence, or climb onto the roof of their little shelter and stare into the distance. He seemed to be trying to understand something, or to be staring into the world beyond, searching for answers that eluded him. He would eat, play, sleep and then go back to gazing into space. With her training in psychology, Lizaene couldn't help wondering what was going on in that little leonine head: his young eyes seemed to be gateways into an older brain.

There was no disciplining of the cubs by a pride male or a mother, so these roles were taken by Cathrine and Lizaene. They rarely resorted to physical admonition; a stern word was all that was needed, and Orva and Omega would generally be on the receiving end of such discipline. Every day the cubs grew stronger and less tired by the tourist interactions, although they seemed to have mixed feelings about visitors. They would either try to ignore them and carry on sleeping, getting slightly annoyed when picked up and petted, or they would welcome the play opportunities the visitors presented. Oliver would get bored first, Omega and Orva played the longest, and Obi looked as if he thought the whole thing was rather silly and that he would prefer to continue keeping watch on the world, alone or with his half-brother.

Christmas and the New Year came and went, and at the end of the holiday season South Africa went back to work. Cathrine, too, had to return to her job in Norway and was booked to leave in mid-January. Cathrine and Lizaene had become very close and they both dreaded her impending departure. As her departure date approached, she spent every spare moment with Oliver and, before she had even left, she was planning her return. She had expected that she would miss Lizaene, Africa, and the animals, but she had not realised the degree to which Oliver had captured her heart. His image was the screensaver on her computer, and she updated it regularly. He was her first thought in the morning and her last at night.

Lizaene had seen humans and animals form special bonds before, and she herself had an innate ability with animals, but she was starting to realise that the bond between Oliver and Cathrine transcended anything she had yet seen. She had read Joy Adamson's books *Born Free* and *Living Free* about Elsa the lioness and her cubs, in which the normally impenetrable barrier between species had been crossed. It was probably too early to make judgements but she knew that Cathrine and Oliver shared something rare and special.

Before leaving for Johannesburg to catch her flight to Norway, Cathrine said goodbye to all the people and animals she could find. She left the cubs till last and, as usual when she entered the enclosure, Omega and Orva welcomed her affectionately and playfully.

Normally Oliver would have been the first to greet her, but today he was lying next to Obi with his little back turned towards her, ignoring her as he stared into the distance with his half-brother. She realised that somehow the little lion knew she was leaving, and tears welled up in her eyes as she stroked him and whispered, 'I'll see you soon'.

She kept her word: her departure marked the beginning of a period of shuttling between South Africa and Norway while she sorted out her life. She returned in March, briefly, and then again in May, this time for good. Oliver sensed each departure and often showed his displeasure, and then was visibly happy to see her on each return. Africa, Lizaene and the lions were now her future, and for a short period she thought she was in heaven. She had no idea that she, Lizaene and the lions would soon be dealt a devastating blow.

CHAPTER 6

DARKNESS AND DESPAIR

It was a cold winter's day in June, and both Lizaene and Cathrine were distraught: their boss had told them that at the end of the week Oliver and his siblings would be returned to where they had been bred.

Staff at Cheetah Experience had assumed that Oliver, Obi, Orva and Omega had a permanent home there, an assumption reinforced by the fact that there were some older lions and other adult big cats at Cheetah Experience that had appeared to have secured a home for life. But the newest cubs were now eight months old and had grown too large for public interaction (petting), so their time as high-earning attractions had ended. Two other sets of lion cubs – Alex and Adamo, Faye and Fundzi – had preceded Oliver and his pride as the petting attractions at Cheetah Experience, and these earlier cubs were also being returned to the breeders. It was a devastating shock to discover that once the cubs were too large for petting and no longer financially useful, they would be sent to an uncertain future.

This knowledge was another milestone on their journey of discovery, and its importance and significance was compounded when their boss announced that no more lion cubs would be reared at Cheetah Experience because it was suspected that the breeders who had been supplying them had connections to hunting.

This realisation came at a time of increased public awareness of the widely condemned practice of hunting captive-bred lions, a practice that had been growing steadily for many years. The breeding farm that had supplied cubs to Cheetah Experience bred large numbers of lions and supplied cubs to be hand reared. Did Cheetah Experience's owners really not know that the breeder was almost certainly supplying lions for hunts? If they didn't at the very least suspect this, they were guilty of almost incredible naïveté.

Knowing that their young charges – their adopted lion children – would soon be leaving and learning that the breeders might be involved in supplying the hunting trade amounted to a double blow for Lizaene and Cathrine. The likelihood was that Obi, Oliver, Omega and Orva would face one of two futures: either they would be used as breeding stock, or they would fall to a hunter's bullet.

Lizaene and Cathrine found themselves unable to block out these toxic and unbearable scenarios. Now the mists cleared, the scales fell from their eyes and they started to look at everything differently.

The days leading up to the despatch of the first group – the older lions – were torment; in some ways time dragged by, but in others it raced. On the Thursday, with leaden feet, they went about preparations for the departure of the first four lions. They were put to sleep with anaesthetic darts and loaded into crates for their short journey into dangerous uncertainty.

Two days later, Obi, Oliver, Omega and Orva followed the same route. However, Obi and Oliver were so tame and trusting that they were able to be coaxed into their crates without any anaesthetic or even sedation. Orva and Omega were slightly more difficult and it took time, patience and coaxing, and in the end they had to be sedated to get them loaded.

Lizaene and Cathrine felt they had betrayed the cubs and, in turn, they themselves may have been tricked or betrayed. As the four 'O's were driven away, Lizaene and Cathrine's grief took the form of a heavy numbness. As the large truck cleared the Cheetah Experience gate and hit the gravel road, its wheels threw up a fine, grey, dust-like smoke, which they watched until it had dispersed and the engine noise had finally faded.

Lizaene and Cathrine now both had a sick, hollow feeling. Before going to bed Cathrine turned on her computer to check her emails. Her screen saver was a photo of Oliver taken only the week before. As his face appeared in front of her the numbness dissolved into tears and she started sobbing. She told herself it was silly; she was a grown woman. Oliver was a lion and that was it; she should pull herself together. But it wasn't that simple. Oliver wasn't just a lion, and it felt as if part of her heart had died – the part that belonged to Oliver.

CHAPTER 7

TREATED AS LIVESTOCK

A week after the cubs had been returned to the breeder, Lizaene, Cathrine and a colleague went to visit them to see how they were settling in. They had been told the cubs would live in a large, purpose-built enclosure; the reality was a shock and a disappointment. The cubs were in a small, cramped pen; the shelter had a broken roof, and the concrete water bowl was dirty, as if it hadn't been cleaned for a day or two. The ground was bare, with no grass, bushes or trees. The visitors were told that the permanent enclosure was still being built, which was why the cubs were in such a small pen.

In some cases, the condition of the animals was not bad, but all too many of them were in a terrible state. Private breeding farms, such as this one, are not subject to public scrutiny. Many breeding farms do run paying volunteer programmes themselves, and are also open to the public on a daily basis – which likely leads to higher standards of husbandry and animal welfare simply because of outsider scrutiny.

Lizaene and Cathrine looked around and saw the brutal realities of captive-lion breeding. They realised these wild species were effectively being farmed, intensively, like pigs or battery hens, with lions and tigers sharing pens both large and small. For Cathrine, in particular, this was her first taste of a brutal reality she had not known existed. What had at first been a bad dream quickly became a nightmare.

The evidence was clear and it all made sense now: lion breeding had become a streamlined process. Soon after birth, cubs would be sent off to an establishment that turns a profit by attracting paying volunteers like Cathrine, as well as charging the public to pet and cuddle the animals. The arrangement works well for both parties: the breeders get their cubs reared by someone else, often for free, and then get them back at a later stage when the cubs' petting days are over – when the next stage of exploitation kicks in.

Lion breeding has become a streamlined process.

The bereaved little group said hello to the cubs they had come to love over the last eight months, and then all too soon were saying goodbye. Four little faces lined up, staring at them as they walked away, and their eyes seemed to ask 'Why have you left us here?' The situation was beyond their control; Lizaene and Cathrine couldn't look back as they walked away because the sadness in the eyes of the cubs was too much to bear. As time went on they would become harder and tougher, but they would never come to terms with the large-scale breeding of sentient, captive wild animals.

Before leaving the breeding farm they sought assurances that the small enclosure that housed Oliver and his pride was indeed only temporary, and that they would soon be moved to their purpose-built new home. The drive from Cheetah Experience to the breeding farm had seemed to take very little time as everyone happily anticipated being reunited with the cubs. In contrast, the drive back seemed endless, and the desultory conversation was punctuated by long silences.

The cubs themselves hadn't looked too bad – but they had only been there a week. What was terrifying was the awful condition of many of the other cats, and the prospect that Obi, Oliver, Orva and Omega could all soon look just as bad. Knowing that the situation was beyond their control only sharpened the girls' feelings of sadness and despair.

At their next visit two weeks later, Lizaene and Cathrine found, as they had half expected, that the cubs hadn't been moved and were still in the small pen. Conditions had deteriorated badly: there was nowhere for the handlers to shut the little lions up while they cleaned the pen, so it was filthy. Old bones, faeces and chicken feathers covered the ground, and the water in the concrete bowl was a dirty green colour with muck floating in it.

Once again, the girls asked when the larger enclosure would be ready and, once again, they were told this would happen soon. The cubs' eyes reflected a change in their mental condition. They had gone from being loved, spoilt and petted to having very little human contact. The keepers at the farm were frightened of the 10-month old lions, and had no safe way to enter the pen; consequently, food was chucked over the fence, which was why there was now no hands-on interaction. The eyes that had been full of fun, security and love now reflected doubt, suspicion and fear.

Lizaene and Cathrine couldn't bear to watch the deterioration in the cubs and, as they were powerless to do anything about it, they stopped visiting them.

CHAPTER 8

MAJOR MILESTONES

About a year later, in the middle of 2013, Lizaene was asked to go to the breeding farm to train the staff to look after the lions. Staff turnover was high and, up till then, no-one had been training new arrivals.

After completing a thorough inspection of the whole farm, she was shocked and depressed. The only silver lining in an otherwise dark cloud was that her former charges didn't look too bad. She got a good look at Oliver, Omega and Orva, but Obi was obscured as he was usually hiding behind Oliver.

Lizaene spent two weeks teaching the staff what quantities to feed the lions, how to feed them safely, how to clean the pens, how to maintain clean water bowls and what health issues to look for, etc. By the end of the second week she was happy with the progress she had made. The animals all looked better, and the staff had confidence and were taking pride in their work. This was a small victory, but all it did was to reinforce the conclusion to which both Lizaene and Cathrine were coming – they wanted to start their own big-cat sanctuary.

By this time, although still only an employee, Lizaene was fully running her side of Cheetah Experience. The owners had given her some animals 'of her own', and it had been hinted that she could run her side of the business as she pleased. However, her initial optimism proved unfounded as the promised autonomy failed to materialise, and by September 2013 her disillusion was complete. She and Cathrine started discussing and planning how they could break free and start their own project.

Only two years earlier, Cathrine had first arrived in Africa as a naïve, raw and innocent volunteer. Then came the hug with the male lion that she describes as 'the hug that changed my life' and, later, the special relationship she developed with Oliver. Now, only 26 months further on, she was planning with her best friend and partner how to start their own genuine big-cat sanctuary.

Oliver before leaving Cheetah Experience

Panthera Africa

For Lizaene the journey had been longer. Wild animals, including lions, had been part of the backdrop to her life ever since she could remember. She had started at Cheetah Experience almost five years earlier, and had passed all the milestones. Enthusiastic ignorance had been replaced by experience and confidence; later, suspicion and concern had crept in, and, finally, a clear understanding of the breeding industry and the exploitation and hunting it led to.

Both of them were unshakably determined – they knew where they wanted to go, they just had to work out how to get there.

In October 2013 Lizaene and Cathrine told the owners of Cheetah Experience that they were looking at ways of opening their own project. They didn't want to let their employers down so they agreed to continue working there while they planned their next move, and would give plenty of notice before they left. It didn't work out this way, because in December they were unexpectedly told they were being given a month's notice to leave. However, by then they had put together business and strategic plans and felt they were ready to take the giant step of trying to raise the capital to fund their own project. Cathrine had family, property and business connections in Norway, so just before Christmas they flew to Oslo with the dual aim of having a long-overdue holiday combined with a business trip to raise money.

For those acclimatised to northern Europe, Christmas must be cold, and there should be snow on the ground for it to be truly magical. Cathrine revelled in the familiar delights of a traditional Norwegian Christmas. For South African-born-and-bred Lizaene it was quite foreign, but an intriguing novelty.

But January was to trigger post-Christmas blues for both of them, albeit in different ways: Lizaene was missing her animals and Africa, while Cathrine was suddenly having doubts about whether she wanted to

return to South Africa at all. The end of their time at Cheetah Experience and their sudden departure had been emotional, traumatic and stressful for both. They had expected an amicable and orderly end to their time at the project, and had hoped to have time to prepare mentally for leaving the animals, but this isn't how it had happened. All the stresses and upheavals of the past months came together to exacerbate their feelings of post-festivity blues.

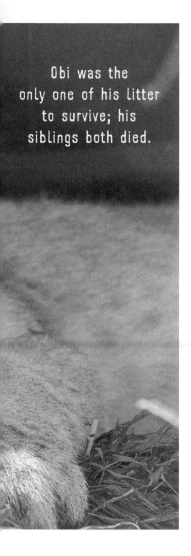

Obi was the only one of his litter to survive; his siblings both died.

Cathrine was adrift on a troubled sea of mixed emotions and, while Lizaene knew exactly what she wanted, she didn't know how to achieve her dreams without her best friend and partner. Her training in psychology told her that Cathrine could only make a considered and wise decision once she had cleared her mind. They took their time, spending a long day talking and slowly unravelling the emotional roller-coaster that had led Cathrine to this point, and slowly the mists of doubt cleared. Just before dark they decided to go for a walk. The snow had turned to sleet and Cathrine decided to check the weather forecast to see if they could expect a dry break.

She opened her laptop and Oliver's trusting eyes stared at her from the screen. The last of her doubts evaporated, tears swam in her eyes, and she no longer cared about getting wet in the sleet. 'Who cares about the weather? Let's go', she said; and, silently to Oliver, she added: 'I am coming back to get you, I promise.'

The next day they fine-tuned their business plan. Cathrine made an appointment to see a bank, where they presented their case and put in a request for a loan. It was declined – they had asked for too much. More fine-tuning of the figures followed and they made an appointment to see a second bank. Again, their bid was declined, but they were not deterred. Apparently they were still asking for too much, so they made more adjustments and arranged an appointment with a third bank. The old adage 'third time lucky' proved correct and their loan was approved. They now had the means to turn dreams into reality and couldn't wait to get back to South Africa.

CHAPTER 9
FROM DREAMS TO REALITY

When Cathrine and Lizaene landed back in South Africa on 4 February 2014, any gloom and doubts they had felt in Norway were replaced by hope and excitement. For months, they had been planning what they wanted to do. They dreamt of rescuing Obi, Oliver, and other needy animals, as well as rehoming those Lizaene had been given at Cheetah Experience. They had energy, experience, passion, the certainty that they wanted to make a difference, and now they had the finance to take a stand against captive breeding and could rescue at least some of its victims.

Their start would be modest, but at least it was in sight, and its success would be entirely up to them. Their dreams could now become reality.

Their first decision had to be where to acquire the land on which to set up their sanctuary. South Africa is a big place and they had the whole country from which to choose. However, the Western Cape was the only province that didn't allow the captive breeding and hunting of lions, and this principled stand appealed to them. Cathrine is a city girl and liked the idea of being close to Cape Town, and both liked the nature and topography of the region.

Having chosen the general region, they started their search. After much searching and many disappointments and setbacks, they found a property near Stanford, which lies between Hermanus and Gansbaai. It was an ideal small farm of 38.7 hectares with a large house on it.

They returned to the Free State in June and visited both Cheetah Experience and the farm where Obi, Oliver and their sisters had been living. They had previously reached an agreement with Cheetah Experience that once they had their own place set up and ready, they could take 'their' animals that had stayed behind at Cheetah Experience when they left.

Anticipation and apprehension were running very high the day Cathrine and Lizaene went to visit Oliver and Obi. Cathrine, in particular, was excited and nervous. She had known Oliver for just three months of his life, and hadn't seen him for nearly two years. Every day since then she had looked forward to when she would rescue him, and he would finally be hers and safe for the rest of his life.

They had been directed to Oliver and Obi's enclosure and, as they approached it on foot, Catherine strained to pick out Oliver's white coat among a large group of lions lying along the fence at the far side of the enclosure 100 metres away. She looked at Lizaene for reassurance and tried to call out his name; the sound that came out was a nervous croak, so she cleared her throat and almost shouted 'Oliver'. A white head popped up from among the group of sleeping lions, and she called again.

Immediately he was on his feet; he ran the whole way around the enclosure and met Cathrine at the fence. By the time he reached her she was sobbing. Happiness, elation, and relief all flooded into her brain and were so powerful she thought she might pass out. Lizaene caught her mood and put a hand on her arm to steady her and share her moment.

Thanks to his white coat, Oliver was quickly identifiable among the other tawny lions.

A pathetically thin, weak-looking brown lion
(Obi) was stumbling across the pen towards them.

The other lions had become curious and came over to the fence to see what was going on, but Oliver turned on them and chased them away. Clearly, he was still the king of his pride, and was now protecting his human friend. While Cathrine was talking to Oliver, Lizaene was looking for Obi. He was not among the group that Oliver had chased away so she looked to the far side of the enclosure where they had all been lying. A pathetically thin, weak-looking brown lion was stumbling across the pen towards them.

Lizaene whistled and called his name and he continued struggling towards them. This brave animal was trying to reach his human friends. Oliver didn't chase him away, and by the time he got to the fence both Lizaene and Cathrine were in tears. But their tears of happiness and relief had been replaced by tears of sadness as they took in the emaciated creature before them that hardly had the strength to stand. Almost under her breath, Cathrine whispered, 'Obi, what has happened to you?' Lizaene knew exactly what had happened and her tears were not only of sadness, they were of anger and regret. She had seen it before and knew that these lions, and Obi in particular, were victims of uncaring, bad husbandry. Unless something was done soon, Obi would become another casualty of captive-lion breeding.

As they said goodbye to the two lions, it was understood that they would somehow find a way to rescue them. Purists would say that 'rescue' was not the correct term, because these lions would not be saved from a zoo that was closing down, or from a private owner who could no longer cope with his toy! This was a commercial breeding facility so Oliver and Obi would have a price tag on them and would have to be paid for. Although money would change hands, the 'rescue' was genuine: had Cathrine and Lizaene not intervened, Obi would certainly have died of ill health or been shot for his bones. Months later, after they had finally fetched their two lions, they heard that all the other white lions at the farm had been shot for their bones only two weeks after Oliver and Obi had left. Had they not been rescued, neither lion would have lived much longer.

The process of getting permissions and licences can take a long time, so Lizaene and Cathrine started talking to CapeNature, the local municipality and others in April, even before their purchase of the farm had actually gone through. By early July the licences and permissions had still not been finalised and the farm's sellers were starting to get restive.

In an ideal world, they would have wanted their licence positon to be regularised before finally signing for the farm. However, the last couple of years had shown both of them that, in this far-from-ideal world, they had only made progress by taking leaps of faith. They took another one, finalised their purchase and moved in. The new sanctuary was named 'Panthera Africa'. The Latin word *panthera* and various derivations are used in many ways when referring to big cats, so the choice of name was wholly appropriate.

A long period of administrative activity and animal acquisition now started. They needed all the various permissions to be able to transport their animals and keep them on their new sanctuary. Since their visit to the Free State they had been talking to the breeding farm where Oliver and Obi lived. In due course, prices for the lions were agreed upon. They also reached agreement with the owners of Cheetah Experience about the animals Lizaene had been given, as well as for others that hadn't previously been hers.

The owners of the breeding farm believed that Obi's very poor condition might be due to his having swallowed a piece of wire. Lizaene and Cathrine had to keep him alive until they could bring him to Panthera Africa, so they arranged a veterinary examination. There was no wire, but he was diagnosed with several serious dietary deficiencies, including an acute lack of vitamin A, which had caused poor bone development and other problems. A rigorous process of supplementary feeding was started to improve his immune system and general condition to boost his chances of surviving the journey to his new home.

In November, the municipality gave their approval, then in December the environmental department objected and said that another six- to eight-month evaluation was necessary. Panthera Africa was on a very tight budget, and sick animals like Obi needed moving as soon as possible. These two factors meant that the proposed delay was out of the question – it could sink the whole project, and might lead to the deaths of some of the animals.

The new sanctuary was to be a not-for-profit organisation that would be funded by paying volunteers and day visitors. Cathrine and Lizaene had spent all of their budget buying the farm, building enclosures and setting up the project. Apart from what was needed to transport the animals, and an amount set aside to feed them at the start, their money had run out. Until the animals arrived and the sanctuary opened, they couldn't generate any more funds. They had come so far, and now it seemed that bureaucratic delays might stop them before they started.

They lobbied and pleaded, and invited all those in the municipality to come to the farm for a meeting to address any outstanding questions. The meeting was arranged, and 10 officials came to inspect the premises and ask questions. The girls had been up most of the previous night trying to imagine all the questions that might be asked, and making sure they had the answers. The inspectors were friendly, but their questions were probing and seemingly endless. By the end of the day Lizaene and Cathrine were exhausted. They spent the evening around their kitchen table replaying the day's events, trying to decide how well, or badly, it had gone. Two weeks later the verbal approval came through, and the licence was issued on 4 March 2015.

They immediately started making arrangements to transport the animals from the Free State, and on 16 March, 15 lucky animals arrived at Panthera Africa – their new, permanent home. They comprised three caracals (Jack, Max and Amy), three fully grown lions (Achilles, Jubatus and Neptune), two Bengal tigers (Raise and Arabella), three jackals (Cody, Maya and Lucy), two leopards (Pardus and Zorro), and the two lion half-brothers Oliver and Obi.

There had been concerns about whether Obi was strong enough to survive the journey, but it was decided that if he died being moved it was better than being shot or wasting away in misery. Oliver had come around from the anaesthetic before arriving and walked out of his crate. Obi was still half asleep and looked weak and dazed, but stumbled out and joined Oliver who was busy exploring the new enclosure.

Although the public opening of Panthera Africa had been scheduled for 28 March, Lizaene and Cathrine decided to delay it for a week to give Obi time to gain more strength, and Oliver time to get used to people again. It was apparent that Oliver had become very wary and frightened of men, and if a man approached the fence Oliver would either charge or run away. An intensive programme of dietary supplementation started, and almost every day there were noticeable improvements in Obi's condition. Oliver, too, improved thanks to Cathrine and Lizaene spending long periods with him by the fence, and his trust in humans started to return.

The opening on 3 April was not intended to be a grand affair, but for Lizaene and Cathrine it was the most important and significant milestone on their journey so far. They still had lots of ideas, ambitions and development plans so, although significant, it was just another milestone – the journey was not over yet.

Sixteen people came to Panthera Africa that day. They first enjoyed refreshments at the house, the girls each said some words of welcome, and then everyone walked the short distance to the animal enclosures.

In the brief time they had been there, Obi and Oliver had visibly relaxed. The little crowd of people stopped at their enclosure and watched them lying together in their shelter. They were both physically and mentally damaged. Oliver was a strong, well-developed lion but had no mane, which was probably the result of stress; and his fear of men indicated that he had probably been beaten and brutalised. Obi was gaunt and weak and not always steady on his feet, but they now shared a new home that would be theirs for the rest of their lives.

Cathrine was asked what it meant to have the animals, and particularly Oliver, at her new centre. She replied with just two words, 'the world'. Lizaene nodded in agreement, walked to Cathrine and hugged her, and a little cheer went up. She, Cathrine and the animals had come a long way together, but this was not the end; it was the beginning of their new beginning!

Rescuing Obi and Oliver meant 'the world' to Lizaene and Cathrine.

PART TWO

Journey of discovery

CHAPTER 10
A FIRST INTERVIEW

The two words 'blood' and 'lions' say it all; put them together and you have not only a powerful campaigning documentary film, but also the shame of a nation on public display, and an indictment of the human race on charges of exploitation and cruelty. The film *Blood Lions* accuses South Africa of these crimes of immorality, and the rest of humanity of being complicit.

The Cook Report's programme, *Making a Killing*, and Gareth Patterson's book, *Dying to be Free*, had both shone damning spotlights on canned hunting in 1997. By mid-2016 I had interviewed Lizaene and Cathrine exhaustively about the story of Oliver and Obi. And I had watched *Blood Lions* (released in 2015) several times – the latest, and arguably the most compelling exposé. I had by now decided to investigate the often-secretive world of big-cat exploitation, and to start my investigations with Ian Michler (the film's leading protagonist).

Blood Lions

Ian Michler

Ian Michler looks like a cross between an explorer and a musician escaped from the Rolling Stones. I consider the Stones to be one of the best rock bands ever, and I have always wanted to be an explorer, so I warmed to Ian as soon as I met him, and had to remind myself that I was there to conduct an interview, not indulge in a happy chat! Below is a record of my ('RP') question-and-answer session with him ('IM').

RP: 'Do you have any idea of the number of captive-bred lions being used for tourism and related activities in South Africa, and how this number compares with the number of wild lions?'

IM: 'Richard, figures are difficult to come by for a number of reasons. The keeper of this information is the South African Predator Association, but not everyone who keeps lions and other predators is a member, and not every member reports reliably. No-one actually knows the real figures; the figure we used in Blood Lions was between 6,000 and 8,000 predators, which includes lions, cheetahs and others. But I suspect it is higher than that – it could be as many as 10,000, with 85–90 per cent being lions.

'There are a lot of people involved who condemn canned hunting but don't want the breeding stopped because they are making a good living out of these lions and other predators.'

RP: 'At the last CITES [Convention on International Trade in Endangered Species conference], COP17 in Johannesburg, the South African government asked for South African captive-lion breeders to be exempt from any lion trade ban, and to be allowed to continue selling lion bones. How did this come about?'
IM: 'People need to understand that CITES is nothing more than a scorekeeper of how well or badly we are doing with this or that species. That is all it is; it is not a conservation agency by any stretch of the imagination – at best it can be described as an organisation governing trade. Many people don't understand what CITES is and have very unrealistic expectations of it. Politics are also involved, so you have trade-offs between countries. Canada, for example, is supposed to be a civilised country, but their voting is influenced because they club 300,000 seals every year; it's the same with Japan and whaling. I don't think that for lions there was ever really any chance of a split listing, and the trade-off was probably that, because South Africa had lost out on rhinos and elephants, they could be given something on captive-bred lions, because it was not seen as affecting wild populations. So, they were tossed a bone – a lion bone!

'The sad irony that was lost on many of them was that only two days before they had voted against any tiger trade, and now here they were opening up a loophole on lion bones that have become the new 'tiger bones'. People also don't understand that even with an Appendix I listing, captive populations are excluded. The EU and the US played it by the book, and because wild lions in South Africa are thought to be well managed and so 'of least concern', and captive-held animals are excluded, why not let South Africa conduct a limited captive-bred trade under strict conditions?

'There is only one answer – we have to stop the breeding! If we stopped the breeding today, we would have 12–15 years for this issue to completely end because that's how long lions live; every single facility would then shut down. The only time we should be allowing breeding is for genuine, repeat genuine, and necessary scientific reasons. Real science is funded outside of tourism and other income streams and is peer reviewed.'

RP: 'Blood Lions has been very successful, so you must be very proud of it! Why was it successful, and what has it achieved?'
IM: 'We understood the power of the visual narrative and didn't shy away from any aspects of the issue. We somehow managed to get interested parties from the animal rights groups, at one end, to trophy hunters at the other, all under one banner. No-one had ever done this before. The film was shown at the Professional Hunters' Association of South Africa (PHASA) AGM in November 2015 and immediately afterwards they took a vote and agreed to support the aims and objectives of Blood Lions.

'Many people had been campaigning against canned hunting prior to Blood Lions, but very few of them, very very few of them, had actually been onto the breeding facilities and hunting farms, and filmed and photographed the extent of what was taking place. I had done that at least 25 times in the course of my work as a journalist, and as a consultant for IFAW [International Fund for Animal Welfare]. We wanted to reposition Blood Lions away from the left wing and towards the centre. It is not just an animal rights story or an animal welfare issue – it's both of these and much more.

'Science, conservation and tourism are all involved and we wanted to talk to real decision makers, so we very carefully chose recognised figures to be in the film: Derek Joubert, Karen Trendler, Dr Guy Balme, Colin Bell, Will Travers and others.

'This film has already been shown twice to the European Parliament, the Australian, Finnish, Swedish, French and Netherlands parliaments as well as the US Fish and Wildlife Service. Governments are a prime target but the general public, the scientific community, hunters and tourists are all targeted by Blood Lions in different ways. This was not an accidental development; it is how we thought it out from the beginning.

Ian Michler during the filming of Blood Lions

'I guess the success is a combination of the visual impact – we didn't compromise on the message – and the way we targeted the message and involved the whole range of stakeholders.'

RP: *'There are around 200 breeding facilities; how many cub petting, lion walking and other similar tourist attractions are there?'*
IM: *'I believe that most of the tourist attractions are involved in some sort of breeding behind the scenes. It's like the zoos around the world – there is a lot of breeding, swapping and trading going on out of public view.'*

RP: *'What would be your theory as to where the wild lion population of South Africa will be in 20 years' time?'*
IM: *'This is the only country in the world where we have three different types of lions. Firstly, we have captive and captive-bred lions, then the wild lions are broken into two: the wild lions that are free roaming, genetically viable populations such as [those living in the] Kgalagadi and the Kruger, and 'managed' wild lions, which are in reserves where they cannot roam completely freely and breed with adjoining populations, so have to be managed in terms of the gene pools, but they are still regarded as part of our wild population. So our wild population is about 2,800 lions, and the captive population may be up to 10,000. The captive population is of no conservation value at all.*

'For lions to have any long-term future on the African continent we have to secure the habitat, and we have to somehow reduce the issues that lead to Human-Wildlife Conflict (HWC). These two things are our greatest challenges, and they are being considered by lion ecologists and genuine conservationists. I don't see lions going extinct in the wild, but all these breeders and fake conservationists are actually muddling and confusing the message, and taking money that could and should be going into genuine conservation.'

RP: 'I guess that breeders would claim to be creating jobs. What's the reality of how beneficial these facilities are to the economy?'
IM: 'Not beneficial at all, they are actually taking away jobs. Some of these places have up to 20–30 volunteers working on their facilities. That property owner is using these volunteers to do menial work on his property and they are paying him to do it. So he avoids having to pay locals and gets paid by people mostly from overseas – it is fraudulent. Why does our government not see that jobs are being taken and stop its support of the breeding industry? It's illogical. We must start asking to what degree corruption might be involved. We need to know who in power and politics is actually involved in the lion-breeding industry.

'At the heart of the issue are the attitudes about dominion and sustainable use. The attitudes have been deeply entrenched in government and the establishment for years, and we now have to try to unwind them. My position is not 'if it pays it stays'; my position is 'if it stays it pays'.'

RP: 'What haven't we talked about?'
IM: 'The whole point, whether it is hunters coming to shoot wild lions, or people wanting to cuddle and bottle feed wild lions, is about this dangerous apex predator. Either pitting your skills against it to kill it, or cuddling it. It has no appeal if you take away the dangerous predator label, so if this breeding goes on, it destroys its own sustainability once the lions have been reduced to being just big semi-domestic pussy cats.'

Michler paused, turned away, looked out of the window at the view across Plettenberg Bay, pushed his hands back through his hair, and turned back to us – 'THESE BASTARDS ARE DOMESTICATING AFRICA'S ICONIC WILD SPECIES FOR PROFIT!' He was as passionate and committed in person as he was in his role as the main protagonist in *Blood Lions*.

CHAPTER 11

A FIRST VISIT

I had heard the case for the prosecution and I believed it. What I didn't know was whether there was a case for the defence and, if so, how credible it was. We were about to embark on a road trip that would take several weeks, cover thousands of kilometres, involve both open and undercover visits – and I intended to use it to test and explore Michler's views and opinions.

I wanted to see, touch and feel this industry for myself, so we left our interview with Ian Michler just before lunch and headed along the N2 from Plettenberg Bay to Knysna, George and then to Mossel Bay. We were booked to 'walk with lions' at a place called Zorgfontein, which is a few kilometres outside Mossel Bay, and where we were to have our first encounters with, in Michler's words, 'lions bred for profit'.

The simple rules we had read on their website were repeated in the briefing when we arrived at Zorgfontein – we were going on the walk at our own risk; participants had to be taller than 1.5 metres; no baggy clothes, scarves, etc., that might attract attention; closed comfortable shoes; and gumboots could be provided if required.

No matter how prepared you think you are, there is something disconcerting, and indeed unnerving, when you follow your guide around a corner, through a gap in some trees ... and find yourself face to face with two adult lions, with no fence between you and them. We walked up and joined the three handlers who were standing less than a metre away from a lion and lioness. Our guide introduced us to the handlers, gave us some rules to follow, and told us that the animals were called Rambo and Gina. We knew these were hand-reared lions, and so were heavily habituated to humans, and we knew they were not supposed to regard us as menu items. Nevertheless, I couldn't stop myself hoping that the lions knew what we knew!

Earlier, when I had met Oliver, his eyes had mesmerised me – they were soft, almost friendly, and seemed to talk. The eyes of these lions were a deep amber colour and, just like Oliver's, seemed to stare right into me. The difference was, there was nothing there – the eyes didn't say anything: not danger, nor trouble, nor curiosity. They were flat, and because they said nothing they were sad.

We set off following Rambo and Gina and their handlers down a track. I could immediately see the appeal of walking with lions. They are the most magnificent animals, and even though these two were clearly well drilled in their routine, and totally habituated to humans, just being within a few feet of a potentially lethal apex predator was undeniably exciting. There were four handlers, all of whom carried big stout sticks, as did our guide, and there was one other paying walker.

We carried sticks as well, which we had been told to take because they would 'help us walk'! I made a point of saying that I didn't need or want a stick, but was very firmly told to take one. I knew from previous research that lions trained to walk with humans are conditioned to fear sticks (by being hit with them when they are still cubs), and so sticks are an effective defence mechanism ensuring that the lions keep their distance.

As we walked, our guide, Mac, kept up a constant chatter, telling us all about lions; but he became noticeably wary if we asked any out-of-the-ordinary questions. We had to be careful because we had been warned that in the lion-breeding and tourism sector everyone knows everyone else; if it were discovered too early that I was an author researching a book, then everyone would be on their guard and we might even be refused entry to further facilities.

We started with simple questions, hoping to steer the conversation into areas of real interest. I don't think that Mac was suspicious of who we were, but he could certainly spot the awkward questions, and these he either deflected with practised ease, or answered from a well-rehearsed script.

Throughout our walk Rambo and Gina went through a routine that was clearly familiar. They didn't need to be told when to leave the track and lie down to provide a photo opportunity, they just did it. Gina knew exactly which tree she had to jump into to secure a meaty reward. One of the handlers carried a bag full of pieces of meat and from time to time

The author at Zorgfontein

these were thrown to the lions. They knew at which places this would happen because they periodically and spontaneously stopped for the anticipated rewards.

At the last photo stop after the lions had lain down, one of the handlers decided to reposition them using his stick, and Rambo got slightly 'naughty'. The guide had only to raise the stick into a striking position and Rambo cowered in evident fear. Shortly after this incident, our walk ended and, followed by their handlers, Rambo and Gina bounded off up a track and over a hill, headed for 'home'.

Three months later I took Denise, my assistant, on the same walk to get her reactions and opinion. We had the same guide, Mac, on both walks but his stories varied. On the first walk he told us the lions had been 'rescued' but would not say exactly from where. On our second visit, he said they had been at Zorgfontein since they were cubs and had originally been 'petted' by paying customers. We had asked on the first walk what happened to the lions when they could no longer be used for 'walking', and he said that they hadn't got to that stage yet. This was in contrast to the answer he gave three months later when he said they were released 'into the wild' on a neighbouring farm called Botlierskop.

I emailed Botlierskop to query this and other issues, and they confirmed that they had a tie-up with Zorgfontein and helped with the retirement of their animals. It is beyond the scope of this book to investigate this situation fully, but for the lions' sake we hope that Botlierskop provides a permanent retirement sanctuary.

After both visits, we recorded our impressions. We had paid R700 each and were told they could take groups of up to eight people and, when busy, did up to five walks a day. Based on these figures we did a guesswork calculation allowing for four, not five, full walks per day.

- 4 walks x 8 people = 32 people daily at R700 each = **R22,400 per day**

Therefore, in a seven-day week the lions are earning R156,800, not including special events, weddings and the profits on shop takings. Of course, these figures apply only to the busy times, but they may not be too far out. An annual figure could easily be imagined as follows:

- 6 weeks of peak time (as above) = 6 x R156,800 = **R940,800**
- 6 weeks of 50 per cent peak time = **R470,400** (weekends will always be busy)
- 8 weeks of 25 per cent peak time = **R313,600**
- 8 weeks of 12.5 per cent peak time = **R156,500**
- 20 weeks of 10 per cent peak time = **R313,600**
- 4 weeks closed

R2,194,900

The above figures are extrapolated for illustrative purposes, but they nevertheless give an indication of what is possible. We did try to get an idea of visitor numbers from our guide, but he professed ignorance, possibly by way of sidestepping the issue. Zorgfontein is well maintained, neat and tidy, which further suggests that a good financial return is being made.

Rambo and Gina went through a well-rehearsed routine.

LIONS ARE DANGEROUS

DO NOT TOUCH

Zorgfontein

Jolanda Schreuder

Altie Clark

The real thing: a wild lion encountered on a nature walk in the Kalahari

Zorgfontein is a slick, well-organised operation. They claim not to be a breeding facility, and currently to have no cubs for petting. The two lions we walked with were in good condition, and we were told that when their 'walking' days are over, their lions will be retired to the sanctuary next door, and not sold on for hunting or other purposes. Even if I accept all their claims to be true, and I am inclined to do so, they are still guilty of turning lions into performers and exploiting them for profit.

We left Mossel Bay and drove east along the N2, retracing our route back to George where we turned off and headed north to join the N1 at Beaufort West, on our way to Kroonstad.

Walking with lions is a lucrative visitor attraction.

CHAPTER 12
WORSE, MUCH WORSE

We eventually reached Kroonstad and found somewhere to base ourselves for our visit the next day to the Boskoppie lion-breeding facility.

Because the film crew had been denied access to Boskoppie, the facility comes across in a negative light in *Blood Lions*. Nevertheless we tried to approach the facility with open minds. As far as Boskoppie knew we were just regular visitors, and so we got the usual tour of what they wanted us to see.

The farm is easy to find. The directions told us to turn off the N1 towards Heilbron, and look for the Boskoppie sign on the right after about 10 kilometres. As we approached the sign we slowed down and had a good look around; I wanted to take some discreet photos before we turned off the main tarred road on to a gravel track, after which a trail of dust would reveal our approach.

We had heard a lot about this place, and none of it was good. We approached the lodge trying to remain neutral, but Boskoppie's reputation meant that we couldn't help being on our guard and looking around with suspicion. There is an excellent investigative site on the internet called 'Volunteers in Africa Beware', and their Boskoppie entry read, 'BOSKOPPIE LION & TIGER RESERVE – One of the worst breeding farms. Owner Piet Swart Jnr was convicted for involvement in rhino poaching. They are selling lions for hunting.' We were soon to see for ourselves.

We met the manager, her permanent volunteer helper and two other volunteers. Soon after our arrival, two very young tiger cubs were brought out, and put down on a small grass lawn so that we could play with them. The lawn is in the centre of the lodge area and is surrounded by guest

Paying volunteers from all over the world come to South Africa to help raise rescued lion 'orphans'. Rearing and cub petting are highly profitable business opportunities.

*Lions, tigers and other predators are being factory farmed
like agricultural livestock such as pigs and chickens.*

bedrooms. We were told that the tiger cubs were four weeks old, and after we had finished playing with them, we were shown into a guest bedroom, which was serving as a nursery for three lion cubs. The baby lions were described as being two weeks old, and the manageress admitted that they had been taken away from their mother at only three days. The little lions were brought out to the lawn to be fed, and we were allowed to play with them. As I held one of the cubs, I thought of Oliver and Obi and their sisters. This was exactly how their lives had started, and had they not been rescued from the breeding farm, their lives would quite likely already have ended.

We asked why the cubs had been taken away from their mother and the answer was not unexpected: 'The lioness would probably have killed them!' Funny how lions have been breeding in the wild for thousands of years and have survived perfectly well as a species without humans having to rescue the cubs. We were told there were three more cubs in another nursery, and these were five or six days younger. Within half an hour of arriving we had met, or been made aware of two tiger cubs, and two lion cub litters of three cubs each. We were starting to see evidence of the first stages of a big-cat production line, causing our tentatively open minds to slam tight shut. There could be no moral defence for this at all.

The next part of our Boskoppie experience was a tour of the pens. At the time of our visit, tours were being offered twice a day at 10h00 and 16h00 at a cost of R150 per person.

As we left on our tour, the three lion cubs were still being bottle fed on the lawn, and one of them was lying beside a half-drunk milk bottle. The image looked irresistibly cute, but I was rapidly learning to see the bigger picture, and to understand the likely destiny of these cubs. Sickening is not a strong enough word to describe the situation.

Our tour was on foot and we followed the permanent volunteer out of the lodge area and down a slope to a lower part of the farm. The first pen we were shown housed 21 lions. Our guide said that 14 had been born at Boskoppie, two males had come from another farm, and the other five were not explained. There was the bloated carcass of a dead cow in the paddock, which so far had not been touched by the lions. The next pen contained 10 males, and no secret was made of it that four of the 10 had already been selected for breeding. What would eventually happen to the other six? A bullet each, perhaps?

We were shown several more pens; I won't describe them all but perhaps the worst horror story was an enclosure in which I counted five tigers and 17 lions – 22 young animals in all. One of the tigers had lost all its fur, and several of the animals were in very bad condition. Stress was evident, their pen was not clean, the concrete water trough was coated with green slime and had faeces and other rubbish floating in it. We were looking at a factory-style production line of a wild species: lions and tigers were being produced like domestic livestock, and words such as 'dire' and 'disgusting' were hardly strong enough to describe what we saw.

Several male lions were pointed out as being breeding animals, and I remember two of them were called Madroo and Mackenzie. In matter-of-fact terms, our guide indicated pregnant females, and explained that they don't 'show' until they are about two months pregnant, and that they produce their cubs at about three and a half months. She described some as 'good breeders' and, when asked what happens to the ones they don't keep for breeding, the answer was, 'The owner sells them to other farms for breeding and other things'. This was clearly not a question she had wanted, and as I didn't want to arouse suspicion, I didn't press the point.

As we passed a series of pens, our guide told us about the lions and lionesses in each one. The pens along our route contained two females, then four, then another four with the male called Madroo, then three lionesses with the other male Mackenzie, then two more females, then a male called Samson together with three females, and the last pen held two lionesses. This made a total of 20 adult lionesses and three lions. This is all we were shown, but there could easily have been many other pens containing more breeding animals. Our guide explained that they always know who has fathered which cubs because they only ever put one male at a time in with a group of females.

Cubs are taken away at birth for three reasons: to provide petting opportunities for tourists and volunteers; because removing the cubs brings the lioness straight back into oestrus; and because hand-reared cubs become habituated to humans, which makes them easy to handle and train. I am sure we were not shown the whole production line, but even based on the 20 lionesses we were shown, the annual cub production rate is significant. If each female produced two litters a year of three cubs each, then a single lioness produces six cubs, which means a total of 120 cubs a year at this breeding facility alone. There is an average mortality rate of 20–25 per cent, so the 20 Boskoppie lionesses we were shown are likely to produce an average of some 93 cubs each year.

In an interview with the South African Predator Association (SAPA) reported later in this book, I was told there were at least 200 predator breeders in South Africa, and there may be as many as 240. One could extrapolate that, if 200 breeders each had 20 lionesses, as does Boskoppie, with each producing six cubs annually, there is an annual production rate of a staggering 24,000 cubs. This is a mind-blowing figure, and cannot be accurate because not all facilities will house 20 lionesses, and not all facilities will be breeding at full rates all the time. Nevertheless, I based my hypothetical calculation on 200 breeding facilities, not the SAPA possible maximum of 240; and if even just a quarter of this maximum number is born, it still indicates a staggering 6,000 cubs being bred in captivity in South Africa each year.

This intensive farming of a wild species is being carried out for three reasons: it's easy to do; it is highly profitable; and – for now – it is legal. In addition to lions, we saw leopards, jaguars, tigers, caracals and other wild species at Boskoppie. We were asked if we wanted to 'pet' two leopard cubs, and our guide was clearly surprised when we said no. Their website states that what makes Boskoppie different to other big-cat projects is that it is 'A family-run establishment, not a commercial organisation, which means that our priority is for the animals rather than for profit'. What we saw was an intensive farming operation that appeared to have profit as its sole aim.

When we got back into our vehicle to leave Boskoppie, and were no longer at risk of being overheard, Jacqui said, 'That was quite disgusting' – which said it all.

CHAPTER 13

UNDERCOVER

I always knew there would be limitations to what Jacqui and I could achieve. We could approach our targets in two ways: we could pay entry fees and be shown around like usual visitors, or we could declare our interest and ask for interviews and guided tours. In either case, we would be shown or told only what people wanted us to see or hear. To get a different perspective and have an inside track, I needed either someone working in the industry to be prepared to talk to us in detail, or someone to go in undercover, posing as a paying volunteer.

Going undercover and maintaining a false façade in 'enemy territory' is something for which secret agents are trained intensively to enable them to cope with all the stresses and challenges involved and successfully and safely complete their mission.

Sending a relatively untrained undercover volunteer into a suspicious target organisation is a considerable risk. As was clearly shown in *Blood Lions*, those involved in the predator-breeding industry are not necessarily nice people – violence and killing are part of their trade; they are, after all, 'breeding for the bullet'. Some of them have convictions for poaching and other related offences, so spies in their midst could literally find themselves 'in the lion's den'. This weighed heavily on me as I debated with myself whether or not to use an undercover volunteer.

Such an 'agent' has to live and project a lie as they play the role demanded by their cover. Every word spoken has to be carefully considered, and if anything is said or done that is out of character, remedial or cover-up measures have to be taken quickly. Before going undercover, the agent's story has to be thought through and thoroughly tested and rehearsed: personal effects, clothes and equipment must all be checked to ensure that there are no 'giveaways' that could blow the agent's cover.

If a stage actor is not convincing in character or forgets his lines, he may get booed by the audience, whereas an undercover agent could face violence or even death.

Sting operations carried out by intelligence agencies, journalists and others are usually quick, short-term hits. Maintaining a cover for days, weeks, or even months is a totally different, and often much more risky type of operation.

After taking all these considerations into account, I still believed I needed an undercover volunteer, but I realised that it would only be fair if they went in with their eyes wide open. All the risks had to be explained.

My research had shown that most volunteers going into this industry are female and between the ages of 20 and 30. I needed someone who was bright, committed, and whom I knew to be reliable. My candidate list threw up an excellent prospect who ticked nearly all the boxes, and at the time I would need my volunteer, this person would be in South Africa, en route to a new job in Zambia. The only box not ticked was gender. This volunteer was a man, so he would stand out in what was usually a woman's world.

James is 32 years old, comes from England, and had worked with me for six years editing the campaigning wildlife documentary films I have produced and directed for Gimme Shelter Films. To an extent, editing these films helped prepare him in campaigning for the rights of wildlife.

At the very least I needed an undercover volunteer to give me a feel of what life is like inside the breeding farms. However, in an ideal world I would want a lot more. I wanted to know what motivated the staff and volunteers; whether they started having doubts about what they were doing and, if so, what they did about it; whether there was evidence of animal abuse or cruelty; and, if the facility was 'open to the public', were there facets of the operation that were carried on out of view, etc.

James and I worked closely together, sifting through a long list of potential lion-breeding targets, and he applied to about a dozen. In applying as a volunteer, he expressed a particular interest in lions, and

The author briefs undercover agent James.

made it clear that he wanted to work with cubs. He finally accepted offers from two facilities, chosen on the basis of their location and being able to accommodate him at suitable times.

James' mission was to gain insight into the way people involved in predator breeding regard themselves and their activity, as well as getting an understanding of how these facilities worked.

My legal counsel advised me not to name the places at which James volunteered. I have taken this advice, and I don't believe that in so doing I have weakened the narrative or detracted from the credibility of the story. Also, for legal reasons I cannot quote directly from the video and recordings that James made while in situ, so I have based the debriefings that follow on recordings he made from memory after leaving the facilities.

We picked James up from Johannesburg's OR Tambo airport and took him to the guesthouse that was serving as our headquarters. Here, we spent two days briefing and coaching him and rehearsing his cover story. He had two target facilities and would spend about a week in each. He had to make his own way to and from each farm so that we could avoid any chance of being seen together and thus blowing his cover.

One establishment was near Vrede in the northeast of the Free State, and the other was outside Kroonstad in the same province. Vrede means 'peace'; we hoped that James' mission would be peaceful!

Neither of James' visits was to yield damning intelligence or staggering revelations with regard to the facilities or breeding operations. He didn't learn an awful lot more by going through back doors than we did by using the front ones. However, by good luck rather than astute judgement we had picked two very different facilities to infiltrate. The farm located near Vrede is owned by a local family who regard the breeding of lions as just another type of livestock farming; they view it dispassionately and run it purely as a business. The Kroonstad farm, however, although it is owned by local people, was being run by two foreign women who had very different approaches from those of their employers, as well as from the Vrede farmers. At this facility, both staff and lions were being exploited.

Facility 1 (F1) is a small breeding facility and hunting farm as well as a day-visitor and catering business; Facility 2 (F2), on the other hand, is a full-scale predator-breeding farm, which also offers various hospitality options on the side.

At F1 the charge for James to spend a week as a volunteer was £1,000, while at F2 it was much less at only R500 per night, making a total of R3,000* for his six nights. By integrating himself into the working life of the facilities and socialising in the evenings, James was able to get valid insights into the mentalities of those engaged in predator-breeding operations.

*At the time of going to press James' £1,000 week at F1 was R18,000, and the R3,000 for 6 nights at F2 was £166 or $220.

Facility 1 (F1)

F1 is reached along a gravel road leading onto a track that ends at the farm and lodge area. There are two enclosures alongside the track, below the lodge, and while James was there these each contained a lion and two lionesses, which were breeding stock. In front of the lodge area were another two pens, one of which contained a male and two females, while the other housed seven lions of mixed sexes.

The lodge is open to the public for drinks, snacks and meals, and visitors eating their sandwiches on the veranda do so only a few yards away from a pen full of lions. James counted 16 lions in four pens close to the lodge. F1 is also a hunting farm so is well stocked with plains game, and game drives are offered to the public.

On game drives, more big-cat breeding pens are visible away from the lodge area, and the following groups of breeding stock were seen, each occupying their own pen: a male and female Bengal tiger; a pair of white lions; two lionesses; a male and female lion; at least 20 year-old lions, and several 13 14 week-old lion cubs. The breeding operation was not as large as the one James would find next at F2, but it was nevertheless considerable.

The dietary needs of 50–60 big cats are addressed by a continual supply of dead chickens from a nearby battery chicken farm, as well as dead cattle and sheep from local farms, which all use F1 as a dead-stock disposal service. Occasionally, game animals are shot for the lions and tigers.

The family running and owning F1 also farms various species of livestock on adjoining farms, and has done so for many years. Their values and instincts are rooted in the past, and they find it hard to understand all the fuss surrounding lion breeding and captive-bred hunting when, as far as they are concerned, their own future as farmers (and as Afrikaners) is under threat. In the surrounding area, violent attacks on farmers are common, and only recently a neighbouring farmer had been murdered. The family members all have licences to own weapons for hunting, and are also licensed to carry pistols and revolvers as personal side arms. These weapons are carried with them most of the time.

James felt constantly under threat at F1 and was repeatedly questioned as to the 'real' reason for his being there. He rode an emotional roller-coaster. The sons of the owner would at times be friendly and chatty, inviting him for drinks, and at others, dark and threatening. Late one night, after an evening of banter that could have been interpreted as threatening, James sent us the (shortened) text message below:

'I'm sorry to message you so late but I am [feeling] extremely paranoid, but maybe without good reason. ... I sometimes [fear] for my life. ... Tomorrow they are taking me out to view ... [a] hunt as [some Americans] are visiting, however half of me is thinking they will shoot me, and claim some accident. ... It is terrifying to think that a shooting or a farm killing could be used as an excuse, so my life here is totally at their mercy. ... That is why I am texting you so if anything dodgy happens ... to me you [will] know how I am feeling ...'

Receiving a message like this concerned me deeply and I replied with words that I hoped would allay his fears and soothe his anxiety.

I believe James' message not only illustrates his state of mind at the time, but also possibly the ethos of the facility and its undercurrent of violence and resentment. The owners' proficiency with guns and their lack of empathy towards the wildlife they were exploiting certainly increased James' feelings of insecurity. Interestingly, James didn't see these farmers as being evil; he could even sympathise with them and their feelings of having lost control of a destiny they had thought to be secure. Breeding lions for their own gain, be it as a visitor attraction, for canned hunting or for any other purpose, was simply a way of earning a living – and a legal activity at that.

To them, big cats are animals just like any other livestock: if they can be easily farmed for profit, then why not? That lions are a wild species is not a consideration; like sheep and cattle, they are bred to be sold dead or alive at a profit. F1 sells mature lions for hunting and the bone trade, and cubs for walking with and/or petting.

At the lodge visitors are offered cub-petting sessions, which are advertised on roadside signs, and which are very popular. James estimated an average of 30–40 people come to pet the cubs daily, with more at weekends, and from what he saw they are a major profit component in the business. In addition to cub petting, there are game drives, camping facilities, hunting, chalets for rent, and catering, and all the business operations tie into the core business of lion breeding.

Because they are conducting a legal activity, in which they see no wrong, the owners of F1 were happy to show James many facets of their operation, including the darting of a fully maned adult white lion, which was either being sold, lent to someone else or transported to be 'hunted'.

James learnt that 70 lions had been shot on the farm the previous year for the bone trade. There was no hunting aspect to this particular exercise – the animals were slaughtered with pistol bullets to their head, just as if they were cows or sheep. I can understand the revulsion this may produce in some readers, but if a farmer regards lions as nothing more than another farmed livestock species, killing them would merely be the harvesting of a resource. And when the lions' time is up, their slaughter would need to be cheap and efficient. In this case the return would probably have been considerable.

It's possible that this slaughter of their stock was related to the mooted ban on all trade in lion products, as was raised at the CITES COP17 conference held in Johannesburg in September 2016.

James was relieved when his time at F1 was up – it had been a real baptism of fire. Over the course of six days he had experienced an operation that reduced the 'king of the jungle' to a livestock species farmed as a tourist attraction. And he had been constantly subjected to suspicion and questioning, as well as being harangued by his hosts about what they perceived to be a decline of their rights and an erosion of their way of life.

Before moving on to the next breeding facility, he had a welcome break in Johannesburg, and he made the most of being able to relax without constantly worrying about his cover being blown.

Facility 2 (F2)

For his next assignment, James made his way by bus to a local rendezvous point where he was picked up by the F2 manager. Although the owners of F2 are also a local family, a couple of women from overseas run the facility, supervising whatever volunteer help is available. On the drive to the facility a series of questions from the manager gave him a foretaste of the suspicion and questioning he would be subjected to for the next few days until he started to gain the trust of the staff.

As they drove, the manager pointed out various features of the farm and she explained the scale and size of the operation. When they arrived, there was a visitor group already there, waiting to be taken on a tour, and James was told he could tag along. Within minutes of arriving he was being shown around a fully operational lion factory farm operating on a much larger scale than had been the case at F1.

On this farm, there is a tree-lined track with enclosures on both sides, which make up the public face of the operation. The tour revealed that F2 doesn't breed only lions: tigers, jaguars, servals, leopards and caracals were all in evidence. In the pens, breeding males and females of various species were named and pointed out to visitors; and predators at various stages of development were also showcased here. These ranged from young animals, only a few months old, to fully adult ones, ready for sale.

James found the tour very useful because he was able to listen to the questions being asked. This not only yielded information, it also told him what type of questions were frequently asked, and what the stock answers were. Among other things, visitors asked if they could buy animals, and the stock answer was that they were only sold to other breeding and conservation programmes. In general, the stock answers weren't just evasive, they were also designed to head off further questions.

Once the tour group had left, James was asked to help with the early evening feed. He quickly had to learn how to bottle feed the cubs, how to stimulate urination and defecation, how to change and take care of their bedding, and how to clean and deal with materials and equipment involved.

Cub-feeding sessions involved all the volunteers. It took half an hour to prepare all the feeds, administered four times throughout the day, at about 8h00, midday, 17h00 and 22h00. It took over an hour for James and two others to feed nine cubs and clean their dens and bedding. He was a beginner, and so had to be shown what to do, but by the end of his time at F2 he had become much faster and more proficient. During his stay he handled lion, tiger and leopard cubs.

James was immediately struck by how much the paying volunteers enjoyed what they were doing. They may have been paying to be there, but they clearly thought that they were being more than compensated by having the chance to interact with the cubs.

During his first cub-feeding session, James realised that his visit was being viewed with intense suspicion. His story was being tested and queried all the time, and if he asked leading questions he could almost feel the tension and imagine them thinking 'Why is he asking that?' The questioning started on his first evening and continued off and on for the next three days.

After the early feed on the third night the two women in charge came and joined him for a drink on his veranda, and for the first time he sensed a changed atmosphere. It seemed as if he had passed the tests and was now trusted, and from then on, he started to learn more and more about what was going on and how F2 was run. However, the suspicion never quite went away altogether, because even after he seemed to have become trusted, he asked more than once for the Wi-Fi codes and was told he couldn't have them. He had told them computers were his job, and obviously they were worried he would hack into their system!

The enclosures at F2, are numbered and James counted up to 21. He believes that the smaller enclosures can take up to 20 animals, and the larger ('wild') ones many more. The total holding capacity therefore is well over 400 animals. However, at the time James was there, the population of assorted lions, tigers, jaguars, leopards, caracals and others was probably about 250, with the breeding corridor and other areas open to public view housing around 100 big cats, and the larger 'wild enclosures' probably another 150. Of these, lions made up some 85 per cent of the total.

In the breeding enclosures there was a small gated pen into which the lions could be lured and trapped should they need to be caught for any reason. These 'catching pens' were often used to trap lionesses while their cubs were removed. The manager made it clear that she wasn't in favour of taking cubs away from their mothers so early, but it was an order from the owners, whose standing instruction is to take them away 'as soon as seen'.

By the time James left F2, the seven cubs he had started with had grown to 12 after five more were born, taken away from their mothers, and delivered to the rearing team in a sack. On his second day James witnessed cub mortality when one of the one-week-old animals died. The women were upset by the death, but the owner's view was that it was an inevitable part of lion farming. The manager said she had once had to cope with a load of 26 cubs, and a male employee said that at another farm he had been in a team that reared 120 at the same time.

As James gained the managers' trust he was shown more and more of the operation, including being taken around much larger enclosures that are off limits to the public. James described these enclosures as massive, and said they contained semi-wild lions and tigers, which are managed differently – in a hands-off manner – from the hand-reared/human-habituated ones. An elevated lookout structure enables animals in these enclosures to be observed and identified. Cubs born in these areas are semi-wild and if they are spotted early, they are taken away; if not, they are left. Cubs not spotted in the breeding areas open to the public, and thought to be too old to hand rear, are also moved to these 'wild' enclosures.

If there's a need to remove an animal from one of the large 'wild' enclosures, a helicopter can be used to dart it from the air, and then a crew enters the enclosure in an armoured vehicle to recover it.

An important part of the work routine is collecting food for the animals. Like F1, F2 also served as a waste-disposal facility for local farmers. Two large battery chicken farms, in particular, phone up every couple of days when they have a pile of dead chickens ready for collection (up to 100 birds is normal). The dead chickens are donated, not sold, as F2 provides a free disposal service. James asked whether, at any stage, the farmers fed their chickens hormones that might end up being taken in by the lions; the question was clearly not welcome and the answer was evasive.

The other regular food source is dead cows which are also given free to F2 by a local livestock farmer. As a general rule, chickens are fed to the younger cats, and to those in the 'wild' enclosures, and whole cows, or parts of them, are given to the adult animals in the breeding areas open to the public. Whole or part carcasses are supplied to the enclosures once a week and are left there. Dead cows are not available every week, so sometimes 10 or 11 days elapse between feeds. Apart from skin condition, which is clearly an issue in captive breeding, from what James saw, most of the animals seemed to be well fed and in good condition.

James reported that escapes at F2 were an ongoing concern, and that the jaguar, in particular, had nearly got out on a couple of occasions. With the lions, there had been two situations when the electric fence had gone down and animals had escaped. On one occasion 10 cats aged 9–10 months had escaped. Six had been found quickly, but the other four had taken several hours to locate, and there had been a huge uproar among nearby residents.

During his time at F2 James assessed the operation as a business model and employment provider, and it looked very profitable. The manager and her assistant were being paid very little; the volunteers worked extremely hard, while paying for the privilege of doing so rather than being paid; and the bulk of the animal feed was being provided free. The basic operating costs are therefore low or non-existent, and profits correspondingly high.

When dealing with living creatures, carers are required to put in the hours necessary to keep the animals alive. Because of their dedication to the job, the staff at F2 were working very long hours, from 06h30 to about 23h00 daily, which would not have been tolerated by less motivated workers. The owner knows this and is successfully exploiting the attraction of working with the cubs.

Because they are working much longer hours than normal employees, and for little or no money, the staff and the volunteers are potentially impacting on local employment opportunities and reasonable wages.

Throughout the process, the lion breeder can capitalise on his stock when and if he needs to, as happened when the F1 farmer decided to 'cash in' his 70 lions. Other ways of cashing in are selling cubs to petting or 'walking with' establishments, or selling adult animals for canned hunting or to the bone trade for their carcass value.

It is difficult to know how much money animals can be sold for at each stage, but males with good manes, which can be sold as trophy animals, can be worth thousands of dollars. I did a web search and discovered trophy males being offered for between $15,000 and $30,000; and lionesses between $4,000 and $5,000. I was told by one source that breeders can expect at least $10,000 for a trophy male, $2,000–$3,000 for a lioness, and $1,500–$2,000 for a carcass for the bone trade.

If the breeder also runs a hunting establishment, there can be a double payoff at the end, because the 'hunter' will often want only the head, and not the rest of the carcass. This means the farm collects the trophy fee as well as the carcass value, and recent US trophy import restrictions mean that whole carcasses are more commonly left by the hunter.

Two questions I wanted answered were: What motivated volunteers to pay to rear someone else's animals? And did they realise that captive-predator breeding involved exploitation and very often an early death for the animals at the hands of hunters, or for the bone trade? James was able to talk to several volunteers and could answer the first question easily. The motivation was quite simply being able to pet and cuddle cubs. There are various reasons as to why this is so attractive: the cubs are cute; they appeal, in particular, to maternal instincts in women volunteers; many volunteers believe the marketing fiction that they are furthering conservation by helping to rescue orphaned cubs; and there's the undeniable thrill of handling cubs that will grow into apex predators.

A more difficult question to answer is to what degree volunteers know or care what the end result is of what they are doing. The manager at F2 and her deputy clearly understood that they were engaged in an intensive farming exercise, and that they were breeding animals 'for the bullet'. Yet they both seemed to have cared deeply for the cubs they had reared in the past, and for those they were rearing now, so how did they square their actions with their consciences?

James believes they deal with this in four ways: they stay in the present and mentally blank out the end result of their actions; they genuinely believe that by doing the best job they can, they are helping each individual animal; the depth of pleasure in the experience (particularly so for broody females) transcends the realities and justifies the situation; and the strong bonds of dependency that form during hand rearing reduce in intensity once the young animals have left the petting stage. Any suspicions that may arise in volunteers about the future of the cubs they are rearing can be dealt with using combinations of the above to blank out the unacceptable.

I had asked James to approach his fact finding and form his opinions with an open mind, which is what we also tried to do throughout our tour. Like us, he started with an open mind, but it didn't take long for the stereotype he was expecting to emerge and his mind to start closing.

He had spent a week in each facility, with a day and a half off in between. By the time he came out of his second deployment, the strain of two periods of undercover work was plain to see.

The information he had gathered about numbers of big cats being bred, and the methods and workings of the farms, was invaluable, as were his insights into the minds of those involved. What he did was by no means easy, and I was not only very grateful to him, I was also proud of him and of what he had achieved.

He left me with a clear message: 'Make sure your book is effective, because I want to feel that I have played a small part in trying to end this evil farming of wild animals'.

CHAPTER 14

NOT SIMPLY GOOD, BAD OR UGLY

Our visits to Zorgfontein and Boskoppie, as well as debriefing James, gave me valuable insights into lion breeding and tourism. We visited a further 15 establishments, and what follows are reports on a small selection that illustrate specific points and varied aspects of lion breeding and tourism.

The website Volunteers in Africa Beware classifies places that employ volunteers as 'good', 'bad' or 'ugly'. I wouldn't argue with their findings or judgements because they are very thorough and provide an excellent and necessary guide, but I have taken a more nuanced approach on the basis that some places may not be all good, bad or ugly.

The Lion and Safari Park — money talks

The Lion Park, operational for over 50 years, was previously situated in the Fourways area and was receiving around 160,000 visitors annually. The Lion and Safari Park opened in its new premises northwest of Johannesburg in July 2016 and claims to be Gauteng's top visitor attraction.

This establishment made the headlines for all the wrong reasons in June 2015 when an American woman was attacked by a lioness through the open window of her vehicle and died of her injuries. This was the third accident at the park in a short time, all involving big cats.

In late 2014, CBS' 60 Minutes featured the Lion and Safari Park in a TV exposé that revealed they were selling lions to the hunting industry. In March 2015, protesters attracted attention around the world when they demonstrated outside the park's gate, protesting at their selling lions for hunting, as well as their offering cub petting to the paying public.

By the time the Lion and Safari Park opened their new facility they had bowed to public pressure and ceased all cub petting. However, money talks, and almost as soon as they stopped these sessions, visitor numbers started dropping rapidly and they suffered financially. I learned from a local tour operator that this establishment had been his top attraction until they stopped offering cub petting. From that moment on, his clients started asking to be taken to other facilities where cub petting was still on offer.

When we visited the park, a large notice outside the gate stated that the new facility was, 'Financed by FNB Commercial Property Finance'. When they stopped cub petting, resulting in a loss of visitors to the park, they would have had to take quick remedial action to be able to meet their running costs and financing commitments – or go out of business. They resumed cub petting and were soon financially back on track. They had learned a hard lesson.

The owners of Lion and Safari Park are ready to admit to mistakes in the past, and now claim to be actively working to stop captive-bred lion hunting and cub petting, and to 'control' captive-lion breeding. Marketing manager André la Cock commented as follows:

André la Cock and Mike Fynn

'Lion and Safari Park management are in fact actively engaged in efforts to put pressure on the government to put appropriate legislation in place to control captive-lion breeding, and in fact to ban lion cub petting totally. You may or may not be aware of the fact that when we moved to the new site it was our intention to not offer any cub petting at all. Unfortunately, the competitive situation eventually forced us to offer petting temporarily to avoid jeopardising the business.

'As a result of this and other factors, we have been instrumental in setting up a Captive Lion Forum in conjunction with the Campaign Against Canned Hunting (CACH). The main purpose of the forum is to come up with solid proposals that we can put to relevant government bodies in an effort to control the industry.

'We have invited several industry players and government representatives to join the forum.'

I interviewed La Cock and his colleague, business development manager Mike Fynn. I found them to be plausible, and believe they were telling me the truth when they repeated the position in La Cock's quote. Until facts prove otherwise, I will take them at their word.

They have set up a group, initially comprising themselves, CACH, the South African Predator Association (SAPA), the Department of Environmental Affairs (DEA) and lion vets and ecologists, to try to find ways of ending cub petting. They hope to attract other interested parties as time goes on.

The Lion and Safari Park admits that, to stay in business at their level, they will have to continue with cub petting as long as their competitors do. In our discussions, we agreed there are three ways to stop the practice:

- Outlaw cub petting – unlikely in the short term because the government doesn't recognise it as a priority requiring attention. Also, it is believed that it helps the economy by generating funds and employment.
- Control or stop captive-lion breeding, which would stop or dramatically reduce cub petting. We thought this was unlikely for the same reasons given in number 1.
- Kill the activity by influencing public opinion: turning cub petting into an activity that people shun and demonstrate against, instead of being keen to pay for.

Given the power and reach of social media, and the increasing number of organisations and voices being raised against cub petting, it may be that in the short term number 3 is the best hope.

One option could be for Lion and Safari Park to work with activists targeting the tour operators who promote cub petting. This comes back to the importance of public awareness – tour operators would have to be convinced not only that petting is morally wrong, but that offering it could adversely affect their business.

Rhino and Lion Nature Reserve – misery and despair

Their brochure states that this zoo-like establishment has a breeding centre, the main focus of which is 'a breeding program for white lions, other endangered species, Bengal Tigers and Siberian Tigers'. By using the word 'endangered', and linking it to breeding, the clear impression is given that the breeding activity is benefiting endangered species.

We visited the 'Animal Crèche', which the brochure describes as 'a nursery/crèche for all young endangered and orphaned animals'. We

What we found were examples of bad husbandry and animal exploitation.

WELCOME TO
RHINO & LION
NATURE RESERVE

found disturbing examples of bad husbandry and exploitation. We had emailed a month before our visit and asked about the availability of cub petting. The reply was as follows:

The entrance fee to the Reserve is R160.00 per adult and R120.00 per child (3–12 years)

We do allow cub interaction when available

- *Cub interaction is an additional R40.00 per person per enclosure to interact for 5 min.*

Currently we have the following cubs available for interaction:

- *6 x brown lion cubs (3 months) – Everyone can interact.*
- *2 x White Bengal tigers (4 months) – Everyone (open for playtime 11.00 –13.00 and 14.00–16.00*
- *1 x Black Leopard and 1 x normal Leopard (4 months and 3 months) only 16 years and older*
- *Anabel the Cheetah (2 years old) only 16 years and older*
- *Cub interaction is available from 10.00–16.00*

By the time of our visit a month later, the animals mentioned above would have been that much older. There was one small pen containing a pair of tiny leopards which, to our untutored eye, looked to be only about six weeks old, definitely not the four-month-old animals mentioned in their email. The six three-month-old brown lion cubs were also not in evidence, and nor were the two four-month-old white Bengal tigers.

What we did see in addition to the leopard cubs were very young lion and tiger cubs being petted in disturbing circumstances. Each time the cubs tried to crawl away from being petted, the handler picked them up and carried them back; they were so tired they were falling asleep while being handled. It seemed that the older cubs mentioned in their email had been replaced by much younger animals.

We didn't enter the pens to pet the cubs, but were able to get close enough to see that most of them seemed to have skin complaints. The baby lions, tigers and leopards were all pictures of misery.

Sadly, our time was limited so we weren't able to explore what animals

The author believes that cross-breeding lions and tigers produces freaks whose only value is commercial. The resulting offspring of such unnatural unions are known either as 'tigons' or 'ligers'.

were in the 'breeding centre', shown on the site map as being near the main gate. We did, however, find several pens housing adult big cats near the crèche. There was a pair of clouded leopards, which are normally found in Southeast Asia and are listed as Vulnerable by the IUCN, as well as Bengal tigers, brown lions, white lions, a black jaguar, Eurasian lynx, a highly stressed leopard on its own, and Siberian tigers.

As stated earlier, the Rhino and Lion Nature Reserve's literature promotes the image that saving rare breeds and conservation are integral parts of their operations. What we observed was bad husbandry and the exploitation of sad-looking animals. The offer of petting, which from what we saw is based on a continual supply of cubs, indicated that their 'breeding centre' is likely to be producing lion and tiger cubs all the time. Notices informed visitors that drones are not allowed. There could be many reasons for this, but one of them might be that drones with cameras attached to them could fly over the screened-off areas and film what happens inside them.

Ukutula – slick, convincing, confusing

Ukutula Lodge and Game Reserve lies northwest of Brits in Gauteng. Compared to most of the other outfits we visited, Ukutula and its owner Willi Jacobs are class acts. Assured, knowledgeable and slick, Jacobs told a compelling story. The set-up at Ukutula matched Jacobs himself: it was smart, well organised and impressive.

When I interviewed Jacobs, it did not take long before he introduced the subject of the film *Blood Lions*. He dislikes the film and its makers with a passion, and believes they deceived and misrepresented him. His dislike of the *Blood Lions* team extends to other conservation activists. He believes that the 'emotion of the conservation and animal welfare topics [in the film] has been hijacked by the activist community to get into people's wallets'. In the case of lions, he claims that activists have coupled canned hunting (in which he is not involved) with cub petting and walking with lions (activities that help finance research, education and his general operating costs); and that they use the animal-rights aspects of the issue to tar everyone with the same brush and, in his case, unfairly attack his reputation.

The clouded leopard (advertised for viewing at Rhino and Lion Nature Reserve) is an endangered species.

A tip-off sent us to Cheetau Lodge, where staff initially treated us with frostiness and suspicion.

At Moreson there is no pretence about breeding lions for conservation or awareness; they are open about their profit motive.

We visited Obi and Oliver's first home, Cheetah Experience.

He acknowledges that he profits from his activities, and sees nothing wrong in this as a lot of what he generates is ploughed back not only into improving his own farm, but also helping scientific research. The list of research projects he claims to have enabled or been involved in is impressive: research into a range of feline issues such as AIDS, tuberculosis, diabetes, dental problems, genetics, artificial reproductive technology and others. At the time we interviewed Jacobs, there was a PhD student doing research into various aspects of cub petting, and she was working both at Ukutula and Lion and Safari Park. Ukutula also has an ongoing research and conservation agreement with a German non-profit organisation called Pro Fetura.

In *Blood Lions* there is an interview with Professor Bob Millar, the Director of the Mammal Research Institute at Pretoria University. Millar was involved in various research programmes with some 20–30 lions from Ukutula – a factor that supports Willi Jacobs' claim. Millar says that he doesn't know what ultimately happens to the lions, but that if he found out that lions were mishandled at Ukutula in a way that he saw as being unacceptable, he 'would have nothing to do with conducting research in that environment'. This is a perfectly reasonable position from an outsider.

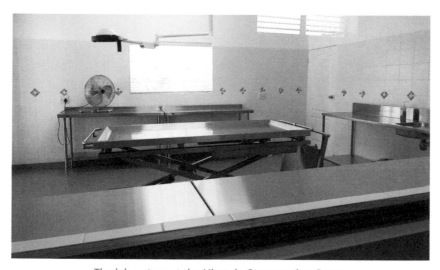

The laboratory at the Ukutula Conservation Centre

Willi Jacobs was keen to show me how different Ukutula is from other lion-breeding facilities. He took us on a short walking tour and showed us his 'Ukutula Conservation Centre', which is an ultra-clean, well-equipped laboratory facility housing some expensive equipment. It was deserted and looked so spotless that we wondered how much it was in current use. If the lab is part of a 'smoke and mirrors' ploy, it is a very expensive mirror, or it may have been used by Professor Millar, Pro Fetura and others when doing research in the past.

Jacobs admits to selling lions, but claims to do everything possible to control the fate of the animals he sells. He claims he researches buyers before agreeing to sell to them, and makes them sign contracts agreeing that the lions will never be used for hunting. In addition, he says he has developed a web-based computer program called 'Eco-scan', which tracks the subsequent journeys of lions he has sold.

In *Blood Lions*, when asked why they were breeding big cats so intensively, a woman from Ukutula claimed it was 'just for the research'. This statement is at odds with the woman's own earlier admission that 'sometimes we sell them to other breeding centres and predator parks'. Jacobs gave me the impression that they don't sell many lions. He mentioned that he had recently sold two to Australia. This is at odds with his admitting to Chris Mercer and Linda Park of CACH that he had sold 20 lions to central Africa – contradictory responses that give rise to a sensation of 'smoke and mirrors'.

Furthermore, I was told by a source that in August 2015 a permit was issued to Ukutula for the sale and movement of 50 lions to a farm in the Free State. Proof of the sale of large numbers of lions would help clarify the conflicting statements made by Jacobs and the Ukutula spokeswoman in the film. I emailed Jacobs to question him about the permit to sell the 50 lions. He did not deny the existence of the permit, but stated emphatically that, in the end, for various reasons, the sale did not take place. In spite of this, the existence of the permit and his admission that he had looked at selling lions both clearly prove intent.

At the end of our interview Jacobs invited me to return a few days later and take part in one of their lion walks, so that I could see how differently they did it compared to others. The only previous experience I'd had of walking with lions was at Zorgfontein, and the Ukutula modus operandi proved to be very different. At Zorgfontein there were two adult lions, four handlers, a guide, only three walkers, and the lions were clearly well trained and performed like circus animals. At Ukutula there were four young lions, two handlers, one guide, and five walkers, and the lions, while clearly familiar with the walk, were certainly not highly trained. They often left the track, ran around playing, disappeared and reappeared, and towards the end of the walk chased a zebra and disappeared altogether.

The contrast could not have been greater. Certainly, the Ukutula experience was wilder and more natural, but I believe that on that walk there was a far higher possibility of an accident. There were more lions, teamed with less discipline and fewer handlers, and in the end the handlers had no idea where the lions were.

On the Ukutula walk there were more lions, but it was characterised by less discipline and with fewer handlers than I had previously encountered. Before the end of the walk the lions chased a zebra and simply disappeared from view.

A young lion jumps down from a tree after climbing it to be given a meaty reward.

Cheetahs are widely used by petting establishments.

Accidents at big-cat tourism centres are said to be common and are often kept out of the news. There have been human fatalities, and there will be more. These 'walking with lions' interactions are not educational, as is often claimed; they are purely for kicks at one level or another. Human death or injury, and the resulting maligning of lions, are high prices to pay for a Facebook photo or a 'selfie'. In the event of an accident, the lions and tourists involved both pay a heavy price, while the tourist operators continue making profits, relying on the signing of waivers and insurance as protection against possible lawsuits for damages.

In the film *Blood Lions*, it is claimed that 25 volunteers generate about $US60,000 over a period of just two weeks. Jacobs strongly contested this, saying that agents take 40–50 per cent of the profits, so even before expenses are deducted, the *Blood Lions* figure is roughly halved. If this is true, Jacobs should have jumped at the chance of being interviewed – an opportunity offered to him by the makers of *Blood Lions* – and his precondition could have been that he be allowed to see and agree on the final cut of his interview. As it is, he lost the opportunity, and so played into the hands of those who claim he is just trying to put an acceptable face on the unacceptable.

Was Ukutula unfairly represented in *Blood Lions*? Are they knowingly selling lions into hunting and for other cruel and exploitative purposes? I don't know. My information indicates the possibility of a first-class example of 'smoke and mirrors', and that Jacobs lost the opportunity of stepping out from behind the mirror and through the smoke when he declined the opportunity of the *Blood Lions* interview.

Moreson – no-pretence profiteering

The Moreson Ranch is near Vrede in the Free State and not too far off the N3 highway from Johannesburg to Durban. A large sign on the tarred road invites passers-by to 'Play with Lion Cubs' at Moreson, and says that this opportunity is only 8 kilometres away, where there is also a pub and grill. At the gate to the farm there was another sign informing us 'This is Lion Country'.

On the way up the drive to the main buildings where the Lion's Den pub and restaurant are situated, we passed pens containing lions. Once inside the pub we bought drinks and went out onto the veranda, where we came face to face with a magnificent fully grown lion only about 6 metres away on the other side of a very inadequate-looking fence. Also on the veranda were posters featuring lion cubs, and offering the chance to meet them if we paid R60 in the bar. We paid and were directed to a shabby green gate, which opened when we knocked on it. Behind the door, in a tiny enclosure perhaps 6 x 5 metres, were 11 lion cubs. As we walked in, a couple with a child walked out, and we found another couple already inside. As we left, a large group of 16 walked in.

Within 15 minutes a total of 23 people, paying R60 each, had visited the cubs. This amounts to R1,380 for a quarter of an hour, so R5,520 per hour. On the basis of a 6-hour day, the cubs earned R33,120 daily, which, for a 7-day week, comes to R231,840. It may be that our 15-minute period was exceptionally busy, but it was during the week, and I suspect that weekends are busier. R231,840 a week translates to R11,592,000 for a 50-week year. Clearly, this isn't possible – or is it? For various reasons this figure is likely to be unnaturally inflated (although it is based on actual observed attendance figures); nevertheless, whichever way I looked at it, the cubs were making serious money for their owners.

The cubs were constantly handled and looked very tired.

We were told the cubs were 8 weeks old and it was admitted that at Moreson they are always taken away from their mothers at birth. At that age lion cubs are supposed to sleep for 20 hours a day. During our hour at the Lion's Den pub there was a continual stream of visitors expecting to pet cubs, which meant the little animals were constantly being picked

The lions were only a few metres away from the pub's veranda.

up and played with. Some of them were so tired they didn't wake up when handled. To add insult to injury, both the floor and their water trough were dirty.

If South African society at large knew and understood what was involved in this profit enterprise, I don't believe they would approve of it. We were told that cubs are petted in the little pen until they are 5 or 6 months old and are then replaced. This indicates a continual supply of cubs, which explains the breeding lions in the pens near the pub veranda. We had seen a male and two females in each of two pens, and a mixed group in a third. The cubs' keeper said there were 37 adult lions on the ranch, so there were a lot that we didn't see, and this probably meant more breeding animals.

The mothers of the 11 cubs in the petting pen were probably already pregnant again, so a total yearly production capacity of 30–40 cubs could easily be imagined, and this is probably a low estimate. I wonder what happens to them? The suspicion has to be that they end up in the bone trade, or are served up for hunting, or both.

From what we saw, Moreson doesn't make any claims about helping conservation or education. The establishment is run solely for profit. And, by not pretending otherwise, they are at least being more honest than many others. Which doesn't excuse what we saw – the sustained abuse and exploitation of animals is surely not an acceptable way of turning a profit in the 21st century?

Cheetah Experience – where the story started

Part One told the story of the start of Obi and Oliver's lives at Cheetah Experience, where Lizaene worked and Cathrine was a volunteer. By the time we visited Cheetah Experience, we had been to nearly 20 other lion-breeding, tourist and sanctuary establishments, and so had seen many examples of the good, the bad and the ugly. Sadly, after our visit we could not put Cheetah Experience into the 'good' category.

Part of a group of 10, we were taken on a nearly 2-hour 'walk-around' guided tour. Our guide was a white-haired man, probably in his late fifties, who not only didn't stop talking, he also had one of the slickest patters I have ever heard. We were charged R120 each for our 'experience', and it was carefully explained that this was not an entrance fee, it was a donation towards feeding the animals. Apparently R120 feeds 'a cat' for 2 days. This blanket statement was one of many that were of questionable logic. Cheetah Experience is home to a wide range of animals: we saw lions, tigers, leopards, cheetahs, servals, caracals, wolves and African wildcats on our walk. To infer that lions and African wildcats cost the same to feed is clearly ridiculous.

Cheetah Experience is not a park; it is a multi-enclosure predator zoo on a relatively small property. We walked slowly while our guide talked incessantly; had we walked faster we could have visited every pen in a quarter of the time. One of the reasons for stringing the walk out is presumably to justify the R120 'donations'. To supplement donations, they take on paying volunteers, they offer adoptions, and they freely admit to breeding cats, especially servals, for sale. Our guide, who had an answer for everything, explained that we weren't allowed to film, photograph or handle some of the animals, either because they weren't theirs, or because they weren't licensed! This particularly applied to some very young leopards that didn't look as old as their purported 10 weeks. An outside source later told us that Cheetah Experience had almost certainly bred the cubs themselves; their awareness of increasing public disapproval of captive breeding probably explains their caginess.

A serval paces its enclosure at Cheetah Experience.

Our guide offered a rambling explanation of why they approved of hunting, but not of 'canned' hunting, and made claims that some of their animals were 'rescued' and then returned to the wild – a claim that was later repudiated by an outside source. The enclosures were often very small, and would be better described as 'cages' – hardly worthy of a rescue effort!

An interesting aspect of the visit was the lack of informed, intelligent questions put to our guide by his audience. We asked a few, but stopped because our questions quickly set us apart. Basically, the public loved the experience, and unquestioningly lapped it all up. This helps explain why these places get away with doing what they do, and points to a real need for more public awareness campaigns.

There was evidence that they were breeding servals, leopards and cheetahs, but we saw no evidence of lions or tigers being bred. In addition to the leopards that couldn't be petted, the cheetah cubs were off limits too due to the possibility of their getting 'infected'.

We knew from Lizaene and Cathrine that, by the time they left the facility, Cheetah Experience had stopped the petting of lion cubs to avoid negative public reaction; but they still like to put cubs on display.

Cheetah Experience is a small facility and, while they admit to breeding and selling animals, they are a long way from the big-cat factory farming we saw elsewhere. Overall, it was not a good experience; but we have seen worse zoos, and were glad to have seen Obi and Oliver's first home.

Zanchieta – a typical small business

Just outside Bloemfontein and only a few kilometres away from Cheetah Experience is the Zanchieta Lodge. This is a typical small business that didn't score any positives but which, from what we saw, didn't score too many negatives either. It is just another of the many places that are open to the public, making a living out of showing animals.

In *Blood Lions* Zanchieta admits supplying animals to the Letsatsi Game Lodge, which is a breeder and suspected supplier of lions for hunting, and they also admit to breeding servals. We saw a pair of light-coloured lionesses, a white lion in a pen with a white lioness (which, we were told, was injected every six months to prevent oestrous, the intended inference perhaps being that breeding was generally being curtailed), two large black-maned lions, several servals, caracals and others.

They claim not to be breeding lions, although they clearly have the capacity to do so. Despite this claim, in *Blood Lions*, a cub was filmed at Zanchieta; and the same woman who had appeared in the film showed

Zanchieta is a typical small-animal-based business.

us around, saying they took cubs away from their mother at 10 days, and bred from their lioness every two years. Then again, the reason given to us for not breeding lions or offering cub petting was that, since cub petting and captive-bred hunting had become talked-about issues, they wanted to avoid problems and speculation that they might be supplying animals to hunts. In *Blood Lions* and during our visit (as evidenced by the above argument), Zanchieta management's statements about whether or not they were or are breeding lions were confusing and contradictory.

At Zanchieta the lions are fed in special pens for public viewing.

Cheetau – perhaps not all is as it seems

The Cheetau Lodge lies near Bethlehem in the Free State. We had been tipped off that there were two Cheetau operations and that they were connected. Cheetau Lodge provides accommodation for visitors only a few metres away from pens containing lions, tigers and other cats, and

A white lioness at Cheetau Lodge

offers cub petting. The other operation, Cheetau Safaris, is a full-blown hunting outfit, and on its website lions were being offered from $9,500, and lionesses for less.

The woman who received us was the one who had been filmed by the *Blood Lions* crew, and who had said on camera that she did not supply lions for hunting. She clearly viewed us with deep suspicion and had a frosty manner, but we managed to ingratiate ourselves with her to the point that she showed us around her big cats. There were white lions, golden lions, tigers, caracals, black leopards and lion cubs. We went into a pen with three lion cubs and our guide lay on the ground while the cubs hugged her, pulled at her hair, and crawled all over her. Two cubs were said to be 5 months and the third, 6 months old.

Our guide told us she has black leopards, which she described as being the most beautiful, but also the most dangerous animals on her farm. She confirmed she was the owner, and showed what seemed to be genuine affection towards all her cats. She repeatedly told us that she didn't supply lions for hunting, but did say that her husband hunted for plains game, and that they had another farm close by. I asked her what happened to the cubs once they had grown too big, or there were too many of them to keep on her property, and she said that some were microchipped and sold, but not for hunting, and the others went to their second farm where the sexes were kept apart so that they couldn't breed.

Cheetau Safaris is also near Bethlehem. Their website displays a hunting price list and is clearly offering a variety of game, including lions, to hunters. I was keen to question our guide about a connection but she had denied supplying lions for hunting, and said she was against the sport; to question her about a connection would just have brought a denial and a return to permafrost, followed by a request that we leave. So instead we bought more drinks and let her talk and continue to repeat her denials.

We left, having decided to find out by other means whether the two Cheetaus are connected. Either the owner of Cheetau Lodge was being – at the least – extremely disingenuous, or it is, for her, an unfortunate coincidence that she shares a name with a hunting outfit.

Chapter 18 deals with captive-bred lion hunting and I will return to the Cheetaus in that chapter.

Three sleepy cubs at Cheetau Lodge

Ranch breeding

As will be seen in Chapter 15, the South African Predator Association (SAPA) believes there is a clear distinction between ranch breeding of lions for hunting, and what they call 'working lion breeding' for petting, lion walks, and other tourism uses. They point out that lions in the former category must have as little human contact as possible, while those in the latter are hand reared and heavily habituated to humans.

SAPA offered to take me to a ranch breeder so that I could see the difference for myself. I agreed that I would not name either the establishment or its owner. Carla van der Vyver (CEO of SAPA at the time) picked me up at my guesthouse in Vryburg and drove me the 200 kilometres to the facility. Much of the drive was on gravel roads, and the breeding farm was a long way off any tourist map.

The owner was standing by his bakkie (pick-up truck) waiting for us, and as soon as I got out to greet him I was aware of the smell of dead meat. The back of the truck contained what looked like half a cow, and a lot of intestines and offal. The owner greeted us effusively; he had been awaiting our arrival before going to feed his lions. As soon as we entered the gate to the lion enclosures I realised that Carla was right: if this was ranch breeding, it was a million miles away from what she called tourism or working lion breeding.

The first pen we stopped at housed a lioness and two cubs. The cubs did not come to greet us; when I got out of the vehicle to take photos they went to the far side of their pen. The lioness paced warily up and down the fence, eyeing us closely. To see what would happen, I walked around the corner of the pen and approached her cubs. The lioness immediately placed herself between me and the cubs and snarled threateningly. I saw three other pens, and the story was the same at each one. These animals were by no means habituated to humans, and behaved quite differently from lions we had met on walks at petting facilities.

Carla had proved her point – there was a clear distinction between the lions in the two types of breeding facilities. It is probable that the ranch-breeding facility I was shown was specially selected to prove the point, but I must assume it was representative of SAPA-accredited facilities.

I have questioned just how significant it is that lions specifically bred for hunting are wilder and less habituated than those bred for tourism. I had seen many very tame habituated lions of all ages (ranging from a couple of weeks to a couple of years old), and certainly shooting them would present no challenge: they were so heavily constrained by their habituation to humans that they were almost as likely to come and rub against your legs as they were to take a bite out of you. The wilder bred animals would probably try to avoid humans, so this, at least, would provide a degree of challenge. But as I thought about the wild- versus tame-breeding question I kept coming back to the issue of enclosure. No matter how wary, cunning and wild a captive-bred lion might be, it cannot escape its enclosure, and the outcome is assured. The hunts are a sham.

Van der Vyver had proved her point – there is a clear distinction between the behaviour of ranch- and tourism-bred lions.

CHAPTER 15
THE REAL SANCTUARIES

As far as I am aware there are currently potentially six 100 per cent genuine non-profit sanctuaries with established track records in South Africa: places that are currently not run for profit, are not breeding, are not using lions for filming or other commercial purposes, and are providing permanent, appropriate homes for their animals. At the time of writing other sanctuaries are being planned, but I have confined this chapter to places with proven track records, and which meet the criteria listed above.

The sanctuaries I regard as 'genuine' are Lionsrock (Four Paws), Born Free (at Shamwari), Panthera Africa (Obi and Oliver's home) and the Drakenstein Lion Park. Time constraints prevented us from personally inspecting and being able to evaluate Emoya in Limpopo and Jukani near Plettenberg Bay. The combined capacity of these sanctuaries is approximately 220 animals, a figure in stark contrast to the thousands of captive lions in the big-cat breeding and tourism facilities (of which there may be some 400) – figures that underline the huge and ever-expanding scale of the problem, and the difficulty of dealing with it.

Lionsrock (Four Paws)

Lionsrock is located near Bethlehem in the Free State and, ironically, was a lion-breeding facility before being bought by the Four Paws NGO. Lionsrock reopened as a sanctuary in 2006 and has the capacity to house around 120 large predators. The sanctuary occupies approximately 1,250 hectares, and has large naturalistic enclosures, as well as on-site veterinary and educational buildings.

Founded by Helmut Dungler in 1988, Four Paws has its head office in Vienna, as well as offices in 13 countries. It is a major campaigning voice in South Africa, and a constructive critic of captive-lion breeding and hunting. Of the four sanctuaries mentioned, Lionsrock has the largest capacity.

Lionsrock – one of the few sanctuaries regarded by the author as being a genuine haven for abused big cats

The genuine sanctuaries must also raise funds in order to cover operating costs.

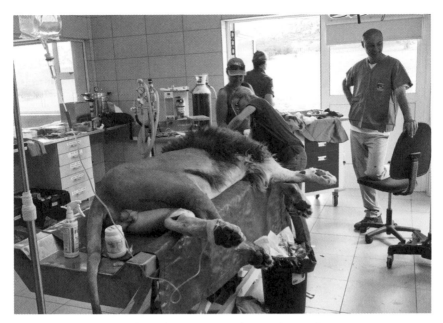

A sedated lion is operated on at Lionsrock ...

... and then transported back to his camp again before regaining consciousness.

Drakenstein Lion Park

Drakenstein Lion Park (DLP) is a 20-ha site located near Paarl in South Africa's Western Cape. The sanctuary is run by Paul Hart and was established in 1998. DLP provides a home for captive-bred lions that have been rescued from all over the world. The capacity of the DLP is approximately 40 animals, and members of the public can help support the park by joining individual adoption programmes. My research indicates that the adoption programmes are genuine, and the DLP is a bona fide non-profit facility, living up to all its commitments.

Drakenstein Lion Park is viewed by the author as one of the few genuine sanctuaries.

Panthera Africa

This facility is featured in Part One of this book. The capacity of Panthera Africa is about 30 animals and there are plans to expand. As with Drakenstein Lion Park, all of my research indicates that Panthera Africa is a genuine not-for-profit operation.

Panthera Africa, the sanctuary established by Lizaene and Cathrine

Oliver before his mane grew back

Born Free Foundation (Shamwari)

The Born Free Foundation was founded by the late actor Bill Travers and his actress wife Virginia McKenna. They were the stars of the film *Born Free*, which told the story of George and Joy Adamson who reared lions in Kenya, and successfully introduced them into the wild; and, in particular, about their famous lioness Elsa. Travers and McKenna became committed conservationists, and their Born Free Foundation is now overseen by their son, Will Travers OBE.

Born Free co-founder, Virginia McKenna OBE

The Big Cat Rescue and Education Centre is a collaboration between the Born Free Foundation and the Shamwari Game Reserve. It is located on the 25,000-hectare Shamwari Game Reserve in South Africa's Eastern Cape. Shamwari officially opened in October 1992, and the big-cat collaboration with Born Free was launched in 1997.

The big-cat sanctuary on Shamwari offers homes to lions and leopards from all over the world and can accommodate up to 24 animals.

If lion breeding were stopped tomorrow, and lions could be neither hunted nor killed for the bone trade, what would become of them? Some could be accommodated in accredited sanctuaries, although these establishments would have to treble or quadruple their capacities to have any meaningful impact on such a problem; others would go to game reserves on which they were not fully released into the wild; and still others might find kindly private owners. But the imbalance between the huge number of captive-bred lions and the comparatively small number of places in sanctuaries may be one of the reasons the authorities are not acting to stop an industry that is fast becoming thought of as shameful all over the world. Who would pay for thousands of lions to live out their natural lives? People often say that they should be released 'back into the wild'. There is no 'back' about it, because captive-bred lions were never in the wild. Although habituated lions have been successfully released, it happens rarely, and is a long and laborious process that must be carried out by experienced experts.

The vast majority of captive-bred lions would have to be shot, and the world's public, led by animal rights movements, would loudly condemn the slaughter of thousands of iconic animals. By not acting earlier to control or stop captive-lion breeding, the South African government now finds itself between a rock and a hard place.

I believe that captive-lion breeding will come to an end in the same way that other repugnant practices have had to stop: when society, national and global, eventually protests so loudly that governments have to act. Because I think this will happen, it is also clear to me that we are sitting on a time bomb, and when it goes off it will be the thousands of surplus lions that get blown up.

Months after having completed our journey, we met our friends Tom, Lisa and Rosie Dawe, on holiday from the United Kingdom, for dinner in Hermanus. They had been touring South Africa for two months, and on their travels from Johannesburg to Cape Town had done many of the things that tourists usually do.

Like children from all over the world, Rosie Dawe
was entranced stroking the lions and tigers.

Tom, Lisa and Rosie had had a wonderful time, and the conversation fizzed as they told us about their adventures, the places they had been, and all the things they had done. I asked Rosie what she had enjoyed most, and her answer was immediate: 'Stroking the baby tigers'. This reaction from a seven-year-old girl clearly illustrates the scale of the problem.

This family had their suspicions when they visited the petting facility near Sun City, and when I told them about the captive breeding of predators, these suspicions were confirmed. They will never visit such a place again and will advise their friends against it. What campaigners have to do is ensure that people like these know the truth and don't visit these facilities in the first place, rather than discovering the truth afterwards, by which time their money has supported the breeding industry.

Dawe family

*The Dawe family in 'petting' action. They now know
the truth and will never visit such a place again.*

CHAPTER 16

THE INTERVIEWS

Our visits to breeding and tourism facilities were interspersed with interviews with stakeholders. The SAPA and PHASA interviews that follow were conducted at the end of 2016/early 2017. Since then, personnel have changed, the relationship between PHASA and SAPA has altered, and attitudes have shifted (see Stop Press, pages 181–183). The interviews below reflect the situation at the time they were conducted.

Hunting of lions is legal in South Africa; 'canned hunting' is 'theoretically' illegal because, at the time of writing, the Department of Environmental Affairs (DEA) had still not produced their long-awaited official definition of 'canned hunting' – nor, crucially, how to deal with issues relating to 'captive-bred' lions.

In terms of rules, regulations and permits, hunting in South Africa is partly dealt with at provincial level, with permits issued in each province under varying criteria, while other issues are decided at national level. Furthermore, the provinces that do allow captive-bred hunting stipulate different intervals between release and hunting of individual lions. For instance, in the North West province it is four days, in the Free State a month, and in the Northern Cape it is two years. These regional variations are all complicating factors in the struggle to regularise the industry, and so harmonisation of regulations would be a step forward.

In view of the varying definitions of 'canned hunting' I encountered in my research (and the absence of an official definition), and to achieve a level playing field, I have produced my own definition: 'canned hunting is the hunting of captive-bred lions in a fenced or enclosed area, irrespective of any other considerations'.

The first two documented interviews below were with the South African Predator Association (SAPA), a predator-breeding association, and the Professional Hunters' Association of South Africa (PHASA), a professional hunters' organisation. Both are concerned with hunting, although at the time of the interviews they had divergent views on crucial issues.

SAPA explained that their members breed lions to be hunted in circumstances they believe to be ethical and defensible. PHASA disapproved of hunting captive-bred lions in any circumstances.

SAPA believes they are assisting lion conservation. PHASA absolutely refuted this, saying the practice offers no conservation value.

SAPA is primarily concerned with advancing the interests of their members, with concern for foreign public opinion being almost secondary. PHASA, on the other hand, relies on foreign hunters, and therefore foreign public opinion was a prime consideration.

South African Predator Association (SAPA)

SAPA was founded in 2008, and in 2013 evolved into the fully constituted and organised body that exists today. SAPA's definition of canned hunting is: 'The shooting of animals in cages or small fenced enclosures where the quarry can't escape and so a kill is guaranteed'. It was headed by Carla van der Vyver – a convincing performer who clearly believed in what she was doing and presented cogent arguments explaining and defending the Association.

Van der Vyver said there could be as many as 240 lion breeders in South Africa, although the generally accepted number is around 200, a figure mentioned in the DEA's 'Lion Biodiversity Management Plan'. (It is impossible to arrive at an accurate figure for the number of predator breeders: during the course of researching this book, figures of between 200 and 400 breeders were mentioned.)

I interviewed Carla van der Vyver in 2016/2017, when she worked at SAPA. She has since left the organisation.

SAPA has some 90 members, and 20 associate members, so if we take the DEA figure of about 200 breeders, then approximately half of South Africa's lion breeders are SAPA members. Since 2015, SAPA membership has grown by more than 50 per cent. Van der Vyver believed this to be in response to threats to the lion-breeding industry as a result of adverse campaigns such as the film *Blood*

Lions, and external decisions that negatively affect captive-lion hunting – as with the 2016 ruling by the US Fish and Wildlife Service, which restricts the import of lion trophies into the United States.

SAPA draws a clear distinction (which many dispute) between what they claim are two very different types of lion breeding: 'tourism' (or 'working lion') breeding, and 'ranch' breeding. Tourism breeding is for petting establishments, for walking with lions, and for uses that require the animals to be habituated to humans. SAPA believes this sector represents only about 20 per cent of the total. The other 80 per cent covers ranch breeding with little or no hand rearing, so the lions are kept as wild as semi-captive animals can be. Van der Vyver stated strongly that SAPA is absolutely opposed to hunting lions that are habituated to humans. Because ranch-bred lions released into large areas can temporarily evade the hunter, SAPA believes its endorsement of this type of hunting is justified.

It did not take long for *Blood Lions* to come up. On the basis of the SAPA distinctions, Van der Vyver believed that the film was one-sided, as it looked at the subject from animal rights and animal welfare perspectives, rather than taking into account resource management or sustainable use. In general, however, her views on the film and its effects were pragmatic and balanced, and she believed it succeeded in highlighting the bad practices that exist in various breeding facilities – although she regretted the impression it gives that these bad practices are industry-wide, which she disputes.

SAPA acknowledges Minister Edna Molewa's statement that canned hunting is illegal, but points out that before something can be enforced in legal terms, it has to have a clear definition – which the DEA had yet to do. SAPA acknowledges that the whole subject is a confused mess that urgently needs clarification and, if possible, uniform rules across the provinces.

The Association is encouraging its members to microchip and take DNA samples from all cubs at birth. This data would be stored centrally at SAPA, and used to manage the lion population belonging to its members. At the time of our interview, Van der Vyver estimated the SAPA lion population to be 4,000–4,500, of which only 600 had been microchipped. Although there is some resistance from members, given the cost of around R2,500 per cub, the target is to have the whole population microchipped and DNA tested within five years.

SAPA admits that there is no universally accepted figure for the total size of the captive-bred lion population, but uses the following overall population figures in South Africa:

- Managed wild lions **800 animals**
- Wild lions **2,400 animals**
- SAPA population **4,500 animals**
- Total captive population incl. SAPA **6,000–8,000 animals**

However, Van der Vyver acknowledged that the captive total could easily be 10,000 or even as high as 14,000, with some 1,200–2,800 cubs being born each year.

Job creation, local community benefits and conservation are all claimed as positives that SAPA members bring – claims that are challenged by *Blood Lions* and others. In particular, its view that breeding lions in captivity benefits conservation by reducing hunting pressure on wild populations is contested by many, including the Professional Hunters' Association of South Africa.

CACH views SAPA's distinction between two types of breeding (ranch versus tourism) as nonsensical, and nothing more than an attempt to put an acceptable face on their industry. Another of the charges levelled against the breeding industry is that lions' genetic diversity is already too low as a result of inbreeding. SAPA claims to have tested their population, and believes there is enough genetic diversity for there to be no inbreeding concerns.

Central to SAPA's position is the belief that whenever there is a demand, a market will emerge to supply it, and that it is better that this demand be met by a well-regulated body such as SAPA, rather than on an ad hoc basis by those who won't observe rules and codes of conduct.

Professional Hunters' Association of South Africa (PHASA)

'The whole hunting industry is under threat in South Africa, and trophy hunting is under threat worldwide because of the reputational damage done to it by captive-bred lion hunting.'

'The trophy hunter wants a memento of the total experience during the hunt.'

'We advocate only fair-chase hunting and responsible and sustainable utilisation.'

The above three quotes come from my interview with Stan Burger, the outgoing PHASA president. The new PHASA president, Dries van Coller, listened while nodding in agreement.

At its AGM on 15 November 2015, a small majority of PHASA members adopted the following resolution:

'At the 38th Annual General Meeting of the Professional Hunters' Association of South Africa the majority of members present voted to distance the Association from captive-bred lion hunting until such time as the South African Predator Association could prove the conservation value of this practice to both PHASA and the International Union for Conservation of Nature ... The then executive committee decided that if evidence shows PHASA members to be participating in the hunting and marketing of captive-bred lion, such member will be subject to the associations' disciplinary processes and may even be expelled if found guilty ...'

Past PHASA President Stan Burger was strongly opposed to canned hunting.

At its later AGM, in November 2017, a majority vote by PHASA members reversed the 2015 decision – see Stop Press on pages 181–183.

The situation in November 2015 was that PHASA condemned the hunting of captive-bred lions as being unethical because they did not believe this type of hunting conforms to the guidelines they follow, i.e. 'the fair chase of a wild animal'. No animal that is accustomed to human movement can be classified as truly wild. One of the points in PHASA's Code of Conduct is that financial considerations should never take precedence over fair-chase considerations. They kindly provided me with the Safari Club International (SCI) rules of fair chase, which include the following requirements:

Dries van Coller was clear that canned hunting was not 'fair-chase' hunting.

- The animals hunted must have freely resided on the property on which they are being hunted for at least six months, or longer.
- The hunting property shall provide escape cover that allows the animals to elude hunters for extended periods of time and multiple occurrences.
- Escape cover, in the form of rugged terrain or topography, and/or dense thickets or stands of woods, shall collectively comprise at least 50 per cent of the property.
- The animals hunted must be part of a breeding unit that is resident on the hunted property.
- The operators of the preserve must provide freely available and ample amounts of cover, food, and water at all times.
- Animals that are to be hunted must exhibit their natural flight/survival instincts.

PHASA's position at the time was one that is widely supported by hunting organisations around the world. Burger and Van Coller were convinced that captive-bred lion hunting has tarnished the reputation of hunting in South Africa and, because of this, 'real, ethical' hunters are going to other countries, notably Namibia, for their sport.

The total membership of PHASA at the time of writing was 499 Professional hunters; 397 Registered outfitters, and 293 Associate, Affiliate, Field and International members. Professional hunters get their first-level licence after attending a 10–12-day course, which is more like a finishing school because most attendees are already seasoned hunters; this results in a licence to hunt small plains game and predators such as caracals and jackals. For a licence to hunt dangerous game such as elephant, buffalo, rhino, lion, leopard, hippo and crocodile, a second, 60-day course has to be attended, and the applicant must prove personal experience in hunting these animals. Hunting outfitters are those qualified to market hunting opportunities and employ professional hunters.

Burger and Van Coller argued that the SAPA claim that they are aiding conservation because the hunting of captive-bred lions is relieving pressure on the wild population is erroneous: there is little if any substantiated scientific evidence to support it, and the claim has not been recognised by the IUCN. They pointed out that, in South Africa, all hunted lions require a permit. Only wild and 'wild managed' lions can be exported to the USA (not captive-bred lions), provided that the landowner can provide an 'enhancement finding' (a guarantee of the hunt's bona fides, etc.) for the population from which the lion comes. In a normal year and on a strictly controlled basis, only 10–15 such permits are issued for the combined wild and 'wild managed' population of around 3,000. There is no way breeding a captive population relieves pressure on the 'wild' populations – the two populations are completely separate.

Before captive-bred lion hunting was fully exposed, there could have been an argument that shooting these lions in South Africa was relieving hunting pressure on wild lions in other countries. Some trophy hunters might have gone for the cheaper, easier, guaranteed result in South Africa, rather than undertake lengthy and expensive safaris in places like Tanzania. However, as PHASA pointed out, this type of hunter is not a 'real' hunter and would have been unlikely to have been in the market to shoot genuine wild animals in South Africa or elsewhere.

PHASA was very clear that there is no connection between captive and wild (including wild managed) populations or the shooting of either category. For Burger and Van Coller the key question was, 'How many unsuccessful captive-bred lion hunts are there?' The answer is 'none'; the outcome is guaranteed, so it qualifies as shooting, not real hunting.

Recently the Safari Club International (SCI) Executive Committee approved a decision by the SCI Record Book Committee that it would require an affidavit for Record Book entries of predators hunted within an enclosure. The affidavit must be signed by the hunter and the guide, certifying that they have met the fair-chase standards for estate animals (see the SCI rules of fair chase listed on pages 121 and 122).

It is estimated that over 80 per cent of hunters coming to South Africa were American, and once the United States Fish and Wildlife Service's partial ban on the import into the US of captive-bred trophies was known to be imminent, large numbers of American 'hunters' flew to South Africa to shoot lions before the new rules came in. The new US law hit captive-bred hunting hard – and with unintended side effects. The high value of carcasses for body parts, mainly the bone trade, and trophy import limitations have led to large numbers of lions being killed by breeders. Carcasses are either exported or processed in South Africa before being sold on. An unanticipated spin-off for South African lion farmers is that captive-bred lion hunters now often leave the whole carcass behind, which is a bonus for the hunting farm or whoever else gets it.

But there was another unintended side effect of the ban. Before the ban, there was an incentive to breed the best-looking specimens possible because they were worth much more as trophies. With a major part of the trophy market now dismantled, the incentive to breed fine-looking animals is greatly diminished: animals bred purely for the bone trade don't have to be good looking – their value is that they are bags of bones.

My interview ended with Van Coller describing a captive-bred lion hunt on which he once took a client, having been convinced that it would be ethical, and that the lion was 'all but' wild. He described how the hunting farm was divided into blocks separated by sandy tracks. The sand made it easy to pick up signs of lions, and when tracks were seen going into a particular block, the hunters drove around it to see if and where they emerged. Once a lion was known to be in a particular block, the hunting party got out of the vehicles to track it on foot, as is required by law. They found the lion easily and Van Coller said the animal they were pursuing looked as if it had a hangover. It eventually stuck its head into a bush, and the resident Professional Hunter (PH) told Van Coller's client to shoot it from behind.

In all, Van Coller attended three hunts presented by accredited SAPA members in three different areas, and will never go on another. He said it was shameful and disgusting, and a million miles from what he considers to be real fair-chase hunting.

Werner Boing

The Free State lies at the heart of lion breeding in South Africa and for many years, until he changed jobs in early 2017, Werner Boing was employed as an Environmental Officer at Free State Nature Conservation. Boing, now an independent nature conservationist, has uncomplicated views and doesn't hide them. He defines real ethical hunting as 'when you walk and stalk and there is fair chase'. Conversely, canned hunting 'is when the animal cannot escape, and is shot in a small enclosure', and he further describes it as 'ridiculous, unethical and [it] does damage to the real hunting industry'.

In 2015, in *Blood Lions*, Boing is quoted as saying: 'On a weekly basis we are issuing CITES export permits for 70–150 lion carcasses that actually leave the country'. By the time he left Free State Nature Conservation in 2017, the issue of permits for the export of lion bones had been suspended pending the DEA's decisions on quota levels. Boing believes the US decision has virtually stopped lion trophy exports to that country, and this and the slowdown in the bone trade has adversely affected breeders. He has seen many farmers selling their stock and putting their farms up for sale, having given up on making a decent living breeding lions. However, he also acknowledges a confused situation, because others are buying into the industry, and the demand for new permits to breed lions is strong. He explains this apparent contradiction by saying that many of the older hunting farmers are giving up, while the newcomers are breeding for tourism and the bone trade.

Although export permits for carcasses were not being issued at the time of our interview, Boing pointed out that breeders seemed to have found a loophole in the laws already, because they were applying for, and getting, permits to export live lions.

Just before he left his job at Free State Nature Conservation, an application was received for the export of 80 live lions to Vietnam – almost certainly to be shot for the bone trade. He explained there are only two key questions to be answered by an export applicant: if the animal is captive bred, and if it was bred legally (i.e. on a licensed farm), export licences are not usually refused, and the applicant does not have to justify the reasons behind the application.

I asked him for his views on the quota figure of 800 carcasses for export, which in early 2017 the DEA announced they were considering, and he roared with laughter. He feels the 800 figure is ridiculously low when taking into account the number of lions being bred in captivity, particularly given that lion bones can easily be processed in South Africa, which negated the need for carcasses to be exported at all. He also reiterated the existence of a 'live lion loophole' in the export regulations. And he mentioned having heard of a man in the North West province who was buying all the tigers he could. The inference was that he was buying lions too, and that both lions and tigers were being processed in the country, and then the finished products sent to the Far East.

Boing believed the value of a whole carcass with a head to be in the region of R45,000, and R15,000 without a head. He shared PHASA's view that captive-lion breeding had no conservation value, and suggested this would only change if there were an accurate stud book to help eliminate inbreeding, and enable genetically valuable animals to be identified.

Boing also shared PHASA's scepticism regarding SAPA's claim that there are two distinct types of breeding. He accepted the theory, but said that in practice he knew of people in tourism who had sold lions for hunting once their tourism usefulness was over. 'What do they do when the lion has no further use? They sell it, and that means it's destined for hunting or the bone trade. Tourism can't take all the lions, and breeders are definitely lobbying for a much higher figure than 800 carcasses a year for export.'

The annual export quota of 800 lion carcasses was later officially proposed by the DEA and is further discussed in Part IV.

This man didn't mince his words. The South African government was now stuck between a rock and a hard place, having let such a large industry develop: there are too many lions and people cannot but be allowed to find uses for them. If lion breeding were abruptly stopped, and animals were euthanised in large numbers, there would be huge animal rights issues.

Werner Boing's opinions were at the time much closer to PHASA's than to SAPA's, and he described the breeding industry as being a real mess. He also acknowledged that the lack of accurate information on numbers of breeders and captive-bred lions, and the confusion over utilisation, were major obstacles when trying to decide what to do about lion breeding in South Africa, and how to do it.

National Council of SPCAs (NSPCA)

The NSPCA was founded in 1955 as the Federation of the nation's SPCAs to provide a forum for ensuring uniformity of welfare legislation and standards. The NSPCA operates on a nationwide basis, working to protect animals from neglect and abuse, and to enforce the 1962 Animals Protection Act, which deals with deliberate cruelty.

As with most other interviews, I started my NSPCA meeting by asking them for their definition of canned hunting. The NSPCA's Cassandra Macdonald's answer was that there was no official definition but that one had been expected from the DEA. However, the DEA had recently decided this was an animal welfare issue and, accordingly, had handed it over to the Department of Agriculture, Forestry and Fisheries. At the time of our interview in early 2017, Macdonald was not sure with whom the responsibility for defining 'canned hunting' rested.

We were joined in the meeting by the NSPCA's Tayla Hawkins, whose prime responsibilities concerned hunting and captive-lion breeding. The NSPCA recognised the need to understand the complexities of all the relevant laws, and so Hawkins' main focus was an analysis of both provincial and national legislation. Once her analysis has been completed, the NSPCA will probably be the only organisation with an across-the-board view of all the relevant legislation.

She said they had 140 breeders on their books and 'were finding new ones all the time'. It sounded as if their eventual number would be close to the commonly quoted figure of 200.

In the previous six months, she had visited various breeding farms and had counted 600 cubs and about 2,000 adults; she could certainly believe the population estimate of 6,000–8,000 lions, and maybe more. Like PHASA and Werner Boing, the NSPCA does not accept the ranch breeder distinction made by SAPA: they believe that ranch-bred cubs are often bottle fed as in tourism breeding, and are taken away from their mothers en masse. And they consider that the resulting production rates of up to three litters a year, as opposed to the one litter lionesses would produce every 18 months to two years in the wild, results in both physical and mental trauma, while poor feeding and inbreeding lead to physical deformities.

As an animal welfare organisation, the NSPCA has many serious concerns with respect to the lion-breeding industry, including cases when hunts have involved animals that were tranquilised, and of lions being acquired by dairy farmers and cattle breeders to dispose of dead stock. Another concern is that there is no legislation protecting tigers because they are not an indigenous species.

They want to see national standards, not only for factors such as enclosure sizes, but also regulating the issue of licences for breeding lions, and the sale and export of animals. Although the NSPCA makes enforcement recommendations, these are complicated by the varying rules and regulations from one province to another.

They had heard of SAPA's plan to establish a DNA database for those lions bred by its members and to microchip the cubs, and confirmed that the NSPCA would welcome such a development. However, they consider that if it happened at all it would likely be a long way into the future.

The NSPCA's in-depth analysis of national and provincial laws, their daily experience in the field visiting breeding farms and other places where lions are captive, and their national information-gathering capabilities all make the organisation uniquely qualified to be part of any in-depth analysis of the lion-breeding industry. This study can't come too soon, and when and if it does, it is to be hoped that government recognises the vital contributions the NSPCA can make.

In this chapter, we have heard opinions from four players in the field and, in an interview in Chapter 10, also from Ian Michler of *Blood Lions*. All five believe their views are correct and defensible. They are all well versed and qualified in their respective fields, passionate in defence of their stand, and while I may not agree with all of their opinions, I have to consider and respect them. I found only one factor that unites them – all agree that no-one actually knows the whole truth about what is going on. Until clear light gets shone into all the dark corners, it will be impossible to make and enforce rules.

Lions are captive bred for many reasons: hunting, tourism, zoo exhibition, private ownership, the bone trade, and others. Whether or not one condemns any or all of these, was and is likely to be influenced by the culture one comes from. A Western European will have a different view from that of a Vietnamese, Chinese or Laotian.

As I identified earlier in this chapter, one of the major problems with trying to assess the lion-breeding industry is the lack of accurate information. The erroneous, the false and the outrageous can all flourish while ignorance persists. A full, independent, in-depth enquiry is needed into the whole industry.

To be able to make any sort of judgement we must ask a question – one that needs to be as universal and basic as possible. It must relate to captive breeding, without which none of the subsequent uses would be possible, and if it is to be a valid question of principle, it must relate to all species and not just lions and other iconic animals. I believe the question is: 'Apart from endangered species being bred specifically for reintroduction back into the wild (e.g. Arabian oryx), is it morally or ethically acceptable to breed wild species for human amusement, consumption or financial gain?' I don't think that, from either moral or ethical standpoints, the answer can be anything other than NO.

For many people, animal welfare considerations will be of great importance, so to end this chapter I asked Fiona Miles from Four Paws to issue a statement on what they consider are the main animal welfare issues.

'South Africa is a country with a rich and diverse heritage, steeped in its iconic wildlife, and a place where many people feel they can come to fulfil their dreams. The lion epitomises this imagery.

Today we find ourselves at a crossroads, both from political and moral standpoints. South Africa has allowed a sordid industry to flourish, built on a foundation of animal suffering, creating an animal welfare crisis that is largely unregulated and growing at a rapid rate.

From an inconspicuous start the local canned hunting industry has boomed, lions are currently bred on more than 200 farms, with at least 6,000 captive lions living under the threat of a gruesome fate – this is a 50 per cent increase compared to 2010 numbers, and growing steadily.

Over the years I have visited many of these breeding facilities and lion parks to evaluate conditions. These experiences haunt me. Basic needs such as diet, veterinary care, sanitary conditions, stress-free environment and shelter are restricted or simply denied. Hearing a wild animal cry cuts through your very heart and soul. I have heard this anguished sound many times as a mother calls out for her cub.

Lying in their own excrement, torn away from their mothers in the first days of life, cubs are manhandled for money. Adults forced to live in unnatural social structures and to breed far more often than can be physically tolerated is heart-breaking. Taking the life of a healthy animal to harvest bones was unthinkable some years ago but now is approved on a quota system.

The profitability of this industry is unquestioned. A male lion with its magnificent mane costs about €25,000, and animals with particularly dark, thick manes can go up to €45,000. It is possible to get a lioness for €5,000 or less. On some farms, even the cubs are offered for hunting!

These majestic animals pay the ultimate price as they continue to live and die in a state of perpetual suffering and fear, fuelled by the greed of a few and the ignorance and moral neglect of many who believe that in some way or another they are contributing to conservation.

The welfare of these animals needs to be put first; if this does not happen we will be left owning not merely an animal welfare crisis, but a completely indefensible disaster, all in the name of greed.'

Fiona Miles of Four Paws

CHAPTER 17

SIGNIFICANT ACTIVISTS

Following the release of *Blood Lions* in 2015, Ian Michler became the most visible standard bearer for those opposed to canned hunting and captive-lion breeding. Twenty-five years earlier, in 1990, environmentalist and independent wildlife researcher Gareth Patterson, who had worked with George Adamson of *Born Free* fame, was busy relocating and rehabituating some Kenyan-born lions in Botswana on behalf of Adamson, who had been murdered the year before in Kora in northern Kenya. It was at this time that Patterson first became aware of the existence of canned hunting through newspaper articles describing how lions were being hunted in the Eastern Cape with bows and arrows. The hunters weren't the indigenous Africans who had hunted lions in this way for centuries. The modern-day 'hunters' were foreign thrill seekers, and their quarry was constrained within a fenced area.

Patterson's preoccupation at the time meant that all he could do was to respond to this appalling news by writing articles in the press. But by early 1997 he was back in South Africa and working with the International Fund for Animal Welfare (IFAW), investigating canned hunting. Through his work he connected with the team that had started producing an episode in The Cook Report series (for the UK's ITV), *Making a Killing*, which was broadcast in May that year.

An audience of 11 million watched *Making a Killing* in Britain, and the programme created a storm of protest that immediately spread to South Africa. Patterson was determined to maximise the opportunity and get the programme broadcast in South Africa and, within a couple of weeks of the British screening, it was shown in South Africa on the popular TV programme, *Carte Blanche*. The response was instant and massive; on the streets, in supermarkets, in pubs and restaurants, canned lion hunting was on everyone's lips. The South African public were astonished that canned hunting was legal, and ashamed that it was happening in their country.

The government moved to ban canned hunting but eventually lost in the courts to an appeal lodged by the hunting lobby. Canned hunting was a political hot potato, with little consensus as to whether it was an issue for provincial rather than national government. Those offering canned hunting kept a low profile for a while and eventually it slipped off the political radar and out of the public's mind. Once the issue had gone quiet, canned hunting expanded again.

Social media didn't exist in the late 1990s. Had this not been the case, the huge public outcry in South Africa that followed the *Carte Blanche* screening in 2015 would have had a far more powerful voice, and there might have been a different outcome.

By the time *Blood Lions* was released in 2015, captive-lion breeding was far more widespread, and was in fact thriving. This was in spite of canned hunting (according to some definitions) now having been declared illegal. The tumultuous public reaction to *Blood Lions* was then boosted by the US government's decision limiting the import of trophies. In addition to the United States (whose hunters represent over 80 per cent of the market), various other governments have moved to

Gareth Patterson

Gareth Patterson's passion for wildlife remains undiminished.

limit or ban the import of captive-bred hunting trophies, and the list of airlines refusing to carry trophies is growing all the time. Those whose proclivities have not been officially curtailed, such as the Europeans and Russians, will continue to come to South Africa to shoot captive-bred lions, and will find ways of taking their trophies home. Although most Americans want the actual trophies, some may come just for the thrill of killing a lion, and will continue to do so. Even without taking their trophy head home, their 'accomplishment' can be celebrated in film and photos of their hunt.

After the murder of George Adamson in Kenya,
Patterson relocated some of Adamson's lions to Botswana.

Making Blood Lions, *left to right: Pippa Hankinson, Nick Chevallier and Ian Michler*

In 1998 Patterson's excellent book *Dying to be Free* was published, and he further emphasised the points made in *Making a Killing*, and presented a strong case for ending trophy hunting altogether. Today, often forgotten and largely unsung, Patterson is still on the scene and his passion for wildlife, including lions, remains undiminished. Towards the end of my investigative journey I went back to the beginning and visited him to get his views on the current situation.

'I think we need a fundamental shift in the attitude of the Department of Environmental Affairs, which seems to be enmeshed with the whole hunting fraternity. Wanting the export of rhino horn, going for an export quota for lion skeletons, and bringing back leopard hunting all indicate that things are not going to change too much within South Africa any time soon. The action is now coming from outside the country; for example, many international airlines now won't carry trophies, countries are coming on board with new rules, and we have seen that Australia, France, the USA and others are all starting to take the right steps.'

Patterson was campaigning from the beginning, and now, 20 years later, I asked him for his prognosis for the future of captive-lion breeding and the hunting of these animals.

'I come at this from the angle of African environmentalism. Most people don't even understand what I mean by the term, which shows how much we have lost of our original environmental cultures. In original African environmentalism, there is no place for killing an animal purely for sport, there is no demand for rhino horn, or ivory, for hardwoods, or for captive-bred hunting. These are all external demands which are far away from the essence of what African environmentalism was, and is, all about. We need a rebirth of African environmentalism, which will say no to these demands from outside. However, as I said there are hopeful signs that overseas countries are starting to take meaningful steps. The 2017 announcement of an ivory ban by China is another such hopeful move, and we must carefully monitor its effects. The world is developing an anti-wildlife-trade mindset, and at the moment South Africa is going against the trend of global opinion.'

Gareth Patterson wants to see a resurgent African environmental attitude that will positively affect African wildlife from within the continent. At the same time, he acknowledges that among the keys to saving wildlife are external actions to reduce demand, and to make supply more difficult and less attractive. Patterson is both an optimist and a pragmatist who believes that eventually, as with many other abhorrent practices, captive-lion breeding and hunting will be confined to history.

Following the broadcast of The Cook Report's *Making a Killing* in 1997, Chris Mercer and his partner Bev Pervan made up their minds to campaign for the abolition of canned hunting in South Africa; and in 2007 they jointly founded the Campaign Against Canned Hunting (CACH). The organisation is a non-profit NGO and no-one, not even the directors, draws a salary. All monies received by CACH are used for campaigning and campaign-related expenses.

Since its founding, CACH has won worldwide recognition and has earned both national and international awards. Bev Pervan's aim was to see the breeding of lions in captivity abolished, and canned hunting banned in South Africa. Sadly, she died in April 2016 before her dream could become reality.

However, Chris Mercer, assisted by Linda Park and many others, carries on the work, and he is determined that CACH will succeed and give Bev the legacy she so desperately wanted.

Mercer, Pervan and Patterson have ensured that the fire lit by The Cook Report continues to burn; and other conservation activists, as well as the film *Blood Lions*, have added to the flames. Gareth Patterson believes that captive-bred hunting will die out simply because, as mindsets and cultures change, the global community will no longer accept the barbaric practice. There are many signs that this will happen, and on a daily basis, campaigners like Born Free, CACH, Four Paws, Blood Lions and others are working hard to make sure it does.

PART THREE

KILL ME

CHAPTER 18

CANNED HUNTING

Widespread use of the term 'canned hunting' started with The Cook Report's episode, *Making a Killing*, in 1997. The expression was in use in the United States much earlier, although the origin of the term proves to be elusive. In the movie industry when something is said to be 'in the can' it is a certainty, a done deal; and prisoners in jail are sometimes referred to as being 'in the can'. It seems possible that one of these might be the inspiration, as a 'canned' lion is both a 'dead cert' for the hunter, and as much a captive as any prisoner in jail. Another possibility is that it refers to something being prepared in advance like canned music or canned laughter.

However the term originated, there is little official clarity on the status of canned hunting, so I asked the Campaign Against Canned Hunting for a statement on the current legal position, as they understand it.

'At the time of writing (July 2017) there is no legal definition of what canned hunting actually is. The Department of Environmental Affairs (DEA) claim that canned hunting has been banned ... on the grounds that any hunt where the permit conditions have been violated is a canned hunt. This could relate to either an administrative oversight, like failing to report the hunt within 48 hours, or to the circumstances in which the lion was killed.

In the court of public opinion and morality, a canned hunt would be any hunt where the target animal is unfairly prevented from escaping the hunter, either by physical (fencing) or mental (habituated to humans) constraints. The DEA cannot accept this definition without admitting that canned hunting is fully legal in the Republic of South Africa. We suspect this is why the DEA chooses to say that only hunts which infringe permit conditions are canned hunts.

Any hunt in which permit conditions are violated is an illegal hunt. To describe any illegal hunt as a 'canned' hunt is a nonsense; quite meaningless. The DEA dishonestly chooses not to understand that the adjective 'canned' is a colloquial expression which means absence of fair chase.'

Two similarly named outfits operate in the Free State, both near Bethlehem, both called Cheetau (see Chapter 14). Cheetau Lodge is a big-cat breeder, open to the public and offering interactions with lion cubs; the other, Cheetau Safaris, has a website advertising hunting opportunities. I had been tipped off that the two operations were connected and that the breeder supplied lions to the hunting outfit. There are connecting points: one is that the person who started Cheetau Lodge sold it to the current owners, before starting Cheetau Safaris; another is that the owner of Cheetau Lodge told me that her husband was a hunter who operated nearby on a second farm. However, I was not able to confirm a current connection. As part of my research I asked two friends to approach Cheetau Safaris, posing as interested hunters wanting to shoot lions.

Captive-bred cubs will almost certainly die early – they will either be killed by a hunter or 'harvested' for their bones.

Captive-bred hunting may have taken a hit following the US Department of Fish and Wildlife Service's ruling restricting the import of trophies, but as the following email exchanges prove, this form of hunting is still very much alive and well. The email replies from Cheetau Safaris make no attempt to disguise that it is a captive-bred lion being offered for hunting and that the outcome is guaranteed. Following all the adverse publicity, I was surprised at how openly the deal was offered.

Email trail 1 (Jeremy Shaw is not the real name of the enquirer)

To: 'Cheetau Safaris' <info@cheetau.co.za>
Subject: Participating in a lion hunt
Dear Sirs,
I live in the UK and have long wanted to participate in a lion hunt. Family and work commitments have not made this possible up to now but having recently retired I'm now in a position to fulfil this quest. I have looked at your website and am particularly interested in the possibility of hunting lion. I'd be grateful if you could email any detail possible about opportunities you provide to do this. I have experience of game shooting in the UK and western Europe but have never taken part in big game hunting before.
Kind regards,
Jeremy Shaw

Dear Jeremy,
Thank you for the interest taken in Cheetau Safaris and giving us the opportunity in making your lifelong dream a reality.
    Can you please just clarify if you would like to hunt a male or a female lion?
Regards,
Carmen

Dear Carmen,
Thanks for your email. If possible I would prefer a male lion.
regards,
Jeremy

Hi Jeremy,

I've attached a picture of a Middle class Lion. The price for this Lion is $17500 US. It includes 6 nights, 7 days daily fees. You can upgrade or downgrade on the trophy, it all depends on what size Lion you want.

The price for a smaller lion is $12500 US, 6 nights, 7 days daily fees included.

The hunt will take place in the North West Province, Kalahari.

Please let me know if you have any other questions. It will be an honour to make your Lion dream a reality.

Best regards,

Carmen

Dear Mr Shaw,

Please see the answers to your questions below in BLUE

Dear Carmen,

I hope you had a good Christmas and New Year.

I'm emailing further to our correspondence in December regarding a lion hunt. I am not quite sure I understand the distinction between bigger and smaller lions and what is involved. Are both the bigger and smaller ones fully adult, and will your guides find a lion in advance according to my preference – i.e. bigger or small class trophy? Months in advance, before the client comes in to hunt a lion, we release 3 different categories of adult Male Lions. When we talk about a bigger or smaller Lion, we are actually talking about the size mane of the Lion. I would like to know if you are looking for a full mane or just a collar mane.

If we have to look for the right size after I have arrived can this still be done in a six-night stay? How we usually work with a lion hunt is as follow: The farm is divided into blocks, not with a fence, but with cut roads. When we get on the track of a lion, we follow it until we can get a nice view of him. If we see that this is not the size of lion you had in mind, we start with another block and track another lion until we find 'your' lion. To answer your question, 6 nights will be enough.

I remain very interested in the prospect of a lion hunt and look forward to hearing from you. Please don't hesitate to email me if you have any other questions or if I can assist with anything.

Looking forward to hearing from you at your earliest convenience.

Kind regards,

Jeremy Shaw

Dear Mr Shaw,

Sorry to hear about your trouble, thanks for taking the time to reply. Please see answers below in BLUE

Dear Carmen,

I have been unexpectedly tied up with a family matter since early January hence the delay in getting back to you. Thank you for your email and apologies for the silence.

Thank you for the information, I will now think about this, make a decision and get back to you. Sorry but [some] final questions.

Obviously I would be aiming for a clean single shot kill, but in case I don't achieve this, what is the usual procedure? We track the lion again and get you another clear shot.

Do I take further shots, or does the professional hunter take over? Werner (owner and PH) will be with you all the way through your hunt. His policy regarding a 'missed shot' is as follow: he does and will not shoot the client's animal, unless the client or his life is in danger. Unless the client prefers differently, of course. He feels very strongly about a client's right to kill his own animal.

I can't remember if you told me where the hunt would take place? On your estate south of Johannesburg or somewhere else? The hunt will take place on our 2nd concession in the Kalahari, North West Province.

Where would I book to fly to? You will book to arrive at OR Tambo, Johannesburg, where we will wait to welcome you at arrivals. From there we will drive to the Kalahari, ± 8 hours drive.

Looking forward to hearing from you.

Kind regards,

Jeremy Shaw

Please feel free to let me know if you would like us to give you a call or if you have any other questions.

Best Regards,

Carmen

To: 'Cheetau Safaris' <info@cheetau.co.za>
Subject: Hunting in Africa
Dear Sirs,

As an avid deer stalker in the Highlands of Scotland, I intend to celebrate my 50th birthday in Africa to satisfy my passion for hunting. What an exciting Birthday this will be for you!! It was interesting when looking at your web site because I thought my budget would only go to Kudu or similar but after looking at your web site, I could be tempted to stretch a bit further to a Lioness and fulfill one of my greatest ambitions.

Could I ask if there is anyflexibility on the price of $7500? We can give you a special price on the Lioness - $6000 US. This will be for the trophy fee alone, excluding daily fees. We need a minimum of 4 days, for the Lioness alone. I've attached our 2017 packages for your attention as well. In those packages, there are daily fees included. If your dream is to hunt a Kudu as well, I suggest you look at Package nr. 1 (which offers) 7 Days with 5 animals included for $4850 US. All we do then, is add your Lioness for $6000 US and then you will have to pay no daily fees. If you have no interest in adding any additional animals, or maybe add animals of your choice, I can work out a custom package with daily fees. The choice is yours and I will help you in any way I can to give you a better price.

As I have never hunted in Africa before, could you advise how many days would be required to be sure to hunt a Lion/Lioness successfully as it's a long way to travel and fail to see a Lioness or similar. I can guarantee you that you will hunt your Lioness.

I regard myself as a proficient and regular shooter with adequate equipment (Rangemaster Stalker Rifle .270 Win with Leopold Match 8.5*50) and of course I would be bringing my own rifle/scope and I have read your information concerning SAP250 which makes sense. We have a lady that does all our rifle permits for us and when you arrive at OR Tambo, she will be there with us, guiding you through customs so that you will have no issues from SAP.

Perhaps you could answer some of the above queries and maybe we can take matters further.
Kind Regards,
Mike Keogh
Looking forward to hearing from you.

Good day Mike

Thank you for the interest taken in Cheetau Safaris and giving us the opportunity in making your African Dream a reality.

Please see below, all answers to your questions in BLUE.

Dear Carmen

Many thanks for your response.

Package Nr 1 appeals to me plus the Lioness trophy, so $10850 seems to be the figure in my mind.

Looking at your package inclusions, you seem to have included everything, so to double check, are any daily fees levied on this above the $10850 ? There is no extra daily fees for package 1, the package is inclusive of 6 nights, 7 days. We recommend that you come in for 10 days, 9 nights for both package 1 and the Lioness ... but there will be no charge for extra daily fees.

I have hunted and know that nothing is normally guaranteed when hunting, and you mention 4 days, and then you guarantee a Lioness.

Maybe I am just a bit cautious, but as I mention above, there is no guarantee normally in hunting but if you make a guarantee, I assume you can clarify that a Lioness can be assured and imagine your guarantee is based on your experience but maybe you could clarify? You are correct in saying there are no guarantees in hunting and I am sorry if it seems like I'm using the word lightly. We have a very high success rate and that's why I used the word 'guarantee'. The trackers we use are very good at tracking lions. Along with Werner and the other PH, you will leave with your trophy.

I only say this because it is a long way to travel and considerable expense, so am just crossing the 't's' as we say. This is totally understandable.

I would be keen to know where we will be hunting and if you can pin point the approximate location so I can see on my map – part of the pleasure of a holiday is the preparation. The hunt will take place in the North West province in the Kalahari.

I would be bringing my wife who is not a hunter, just a bystander and assume this is not a problem. This is no problem at all, she will just be paying daily fees of $150 US per night.

Kind Regards

Mike

Again, very sorry that my previous correspondence did not reach you. Please let me know if this email finds you well and please don't hesitate to let me know if you have any other questions.

Best Regards

Carmen

The guarantees given in the email trails prove that the lions being offered are 'sitting ducks' – they cannot but be captive bred.

Captive breeding
followed by captive
hunting guarantees the
success of canned hunts.

CHAPTER 19
LION HUNT

SAPA invited me to attend a ranch-bred lion hunt as an observer. This chapter should have told the story of that hunt. However, at the last minute, the client (a paying hunter) withdrew permission for me to be present. Given the global furore following the shooting in Zimbabwe of the lion Cecil, and other similar incidents, I was not surprised when the hunter decided against my presence. Indeed, it had surprised me when SAPA suggested I accompany a hunt in the first place.

The lion raised his head and watched them go.

What follows is based on a visit to an actual hunting enclosure, and on detailed descriptions of how hunts are conducted, according to interviews with hunters and filmed material. It has been checked for authenticity by professional hunters.

Dawn was breaking and the sociable weavers were busy coming and going from their huge communal nest. They were taking no notice of the large tawny body stretched out beneath them. The magnificent black-maned lion had only recently lain down after a night spent unsuccessfully trying to hunt. This lion had been born in captivity and taken away from his mother at birth, and from then on had relied on humans for his meals. He had never learned the necessary hunting skills in order to feed himself, so all he could do now was to tap into his instinct. During the night, he had stalked and charged oryx (gemsbok), wildebeest and springbok and they had all evaded him easily.

Three days ago, he had woken up in a strange place, and had been intimidated when a small group of buffalo sensed that he wasn't the threat he appeared to be and charged him. The lion had never faced a situation like that before, and had narrowly dodged the horns of an angry old bull. Unlike secure and content lions, which in natural circumstances spend a lot of their time sleeping, he had been awake most of the time since his arrival as he wandered about, searching for anything familiar. Now, tired and confused, he finally fell asleep.

The lion had been released onto a hunting farm north of Kuruman near the border with Botswana in South Africa's North West Province. He had been moved in two stages from a lion-breeding farm in the Free State, after someone in a foreign land had chosen his photo on the website of a hunting organisation, and bought the right to kill him.

The couple had undertaken the long flight from America in a state of considerable excitement. At breakfast two weeks earlier, the man's wife had

147

insisted he open an envelope. Inside was a card that said 'Happy birthday', two e-tickets for flights to Johannesburg, and some literature featuring photos of a lion. He smiled and shook his head while she watched him expectantly. 'Say something, darling; you have always wanted to do it, and now you will have the chance.' His wife had bought two air tickets to Africa, and booked a hunt on which her husband could shoot a lion. She hadn't really known what she was doing, but the hunting company in South Africa had been most helpful, had even assisted her in choosing a lion, and given her a discount.

He stood up and, wearing a huge grin, embraced his wife. 'Thank you, thank you, I never expected this. I was beginning to think I would never get to Africa.' He had been given a .22 rifle by his father when he was 14, and had been killing animals on and off throughout his life. He had often boasted that the ultimate would be to go to Africa and hunt a lion.

Now, a couple of weeks later, they were at Johannesburg's OR Tambo airport terminal, where they were met by a man holding up a board with their names on it. He was dressed from head to toe in safari kit topped off by a beaten-up old hat above a deeply tanned face. George and Hilary introduced themselves to Kobus from the hunting company, known as 'outfitters' in South Africa; he would be their guide while they were in the country.

George had decided against bringing his own gun and had gratefully accepted the company's offer of a weapon because it meant he could avoid all the complications involved in transporting a firearm halfway around the world. He had been advised to use a calibre .375, and would practise with the rifle, and sight it in before going on his hunt.

Kobus drove George and Hilary to their hotel, where they spent their first night dreaming of their African adventure. They were taken sightseeing the next day with a driver who had been arranged by Kobus; and the following day found themselves in Kobus's Toyota Land Cruiser, heading northwest towards George's date with his lion. In the days since that breakfast when he had opened the envelope, Africa and his lion hunt had been in George's mind almost continuously. It was a four-hour drive to the hunting farm, and George and Hilary were entranced the whole way as they listened to Kobus chatting about the route they were taking and the features along it. The landscape had a stark, harsh beauty to it and Hilary drank in every detail. Although not a great fan of hunting, Hilary had grown up on a farm, and accepted the births and deaths of animals as part of the natural rhythms of life. Her father had shot birds and larger game for the table, and he and her husband had often hunted together. If hunting made George happy, she would not object.

As they sped across the savanna grasslands, George only half listened to Kobus's almost incessant chatter. His thoughts were on the day after tomorrow when he would hunt his lion. He knew his chosen specimen had been bred in captivity, and so was not truly wild. Since Hilary had given him his birthday present he had done considerable research to make sure he would be taking part in a real hunt, rather than a canned hunt. He had had an extensive email exchange with the outfitter, and it seemed that more by luck than informed judgement, she had chosen a reputable organisation offering ethical hunts. He had been assured that, although the lion had been born on a breeding farm, it had not been hand reared and had never been habituated to human contact. They would hunt the lion in a 2,000-hectare enclosure and, although ultimately it could not escape, it could run and hide and give him a true hunter's chase. This was what he had been told and he wanted to believe it, but he couldn't shake off the nagging doubt that, ultimately, he was shooting an animal in an enclosed area from which there was no escape.

Pieter du Toit, who would be responsible for taking George to shoot his lion, was in his early 30s and had been a professional hunter (PH) all his working life. He was self-employed and worked regularly for half a dozen farms and hunting companies that hired him to accompany their clients.

In Pieter's opinion, canned hunting was the shooting of lions in small enclosures from which they couldn't escape. However, tracking an animal in 2,000 hectares of bush (albeit with a fence around it) was, in his view, not canned hunting. He acknowledged that this was not proper fair-chase hunting of a wild animal in a wild place, but these jobs were part of his living, and were perfectly legal. He was a regular at the farm to which he was headed, and knew the 2,000-hectare hunting enclosure well. He lived in Kimberley and had started off on the R31 heading for Kuruman; then beyond Kuruman he drove west for a short distance on the N14 before turning off onto a gravel road on which he would travel for 200 kilometres to reach the hunting farm.

It was Monday, and Pieter had confidently told his wife he would be home by Thursday evening. (He had rarely failed to find, and so thwart his client's wish to shoot, a designated lion in a single day.) He would meet the client at the farm's lodge tonight, and tomorrow they would sight in the rifle to be used, and discuss the hunt. The client he was heading to meet was an American and, in his experience, Americans could be very generous with a bonus payment or tip at the end of a successful hunt. He'd once had a client from Abu Dhabi who had been so pleased to kill a lion that he had given Pieter a $20,000 cash bonus, but this was exceptional; generally speaking, Americans were the best payers.

When they left the tarred road, Kobus announced that they were nearly there and had less than 200 kilometres to drive. Hilary groaned inwardly; Kobus's chatter had slowed and then dried up about an hour ago, and while she was dreaming of her next cup of coffee, George struggled with conflicting worries and thoughts. He was sure they would find a lion – that had been guaranteed. But would he kill it cleanly with his first shot? Would he acquit himself with glory or make a fool of himself? Even though captive bred, would the quarry be dangerous? Would it charge them? And if he didn't kill it with his first shot, would they have to track a wounded animal into the bush? George had only ever shot for the table, and had killed various species of fowl, game birds, deer and antelope. He knew he was a good shot, but what would it be like to look down the barrel of his rifle at a lion?

He realised his palms were sweating. Kobus broke the silence, pointing at a thatched roof in the distance: 'There we are, folks, up ahead on the left, home sweet home'. Minutes later they turned off onto a side track, and approached the lodge that would be their base for George's hunt.

The sound of their vehicle had alerted the farm's owner, who was sitting outside the lodge chatting to Pieter. Kobus braked to a sudden halt to avoid a farm dog that had come to greet them, skidding to a stop in a cloud of dust. As Pieter and the farm's owner strode towards the vehicle, the guests took stock of their hosts: a solid, athletic-looking young man of about 30, wearing khaki shorts, an olive-green shirt, hiking boots and a wide-brimmed hat – clearly the Professional Hunter. The other man was at least 20 years older and, although light on his feet, carried one of the biggest bellies they had ever seen. The older man had his hand out and was wearing a large grin as he approached George. A man in a man's world, decided Hilary. 'Welcome George, welcome, we have been looking forward to meeting you. This is Pieter, who is your PH, and I am André. It's good to have you here.' Pieter also shook George's hand. 'George, it's good to meet you'. Then, almost as an afterthought, André and Pieter turned to Hilary. 'What a wonderful present you have arranged for George; we are here to make his dream come true. Leave your bags, they will be taken to the chalet, let's get you something to eat and drink.' Kobus had been helping a staff member unload the suitcases, and now joined them as they headed for the main building, one of several arranged in a semicircle around a concrete structure with a fire burning in it.

The lodge was basic and simple but adequate. The main building contained the bar, a lounge area, a dining section and toilets, and outside were six chalets. Over refreshments, André suggested that the guests shower and freshen up, and then meet in the braai (BBQ) area for a drink before dinner. André took pride in showing them the large, purpose-built braai near to where the fire burned, and telling them that later they would 'eat meat'. There was real enthusiasm in the way André talked about eating meat, and his huge belly was testament to over-consumption of what was clearly his favourite food.

Their chalet was hardly luxurious but everything worked and the shower pressure was a delight. George had been quiet for the last half of the drive, and because she knew him so well, Hilary knew something was troubling him. While they were alone in their chalet she asked him if anything was wrong, and he answered with a brief 'No, everything's fine, I guess maybe I'm nervous, I just want everything to go OK'.

Darkness had fallen by the time they joined André, Kobus, Pieter and André's wife Marie, who were already sitting around the fire in camping chairs. Their conversation drifted into the darkness, joining the faint distant hum of a generator as they chatted, with the firelight playing on their faces. Apart from George's slightly sombre mood – possibly presaging his later reaction to the hunt – Hilary felt wonderful: they were miles from anywhere, in a remote place, in wildest Africa. There was nowhere else on the planet she would rather be.

For André *braaiing* was almost a religion. He was solicitous over exactly how everyone wanted their steaks cooked, and had already cooked some very tasty spicy sausages, which he said were 'just to get things started'. Marie was a delight – she had an infectious laugh and spent the evening quizzing Hilary about life in America. Meanwhile, André and Pieter talked with George, probing for information about his experience with guns and hunting. George was not the world's most experienced predator hunter, but he had grown up with firearms, and had done a stint in the US Army, so his knowledge of sporting and infantry weapons was extensive and impressive.

With the flames from the fire keeping the cold at bay and illuminating their faces, André gave his visitors a full briefing about what the hunt would entail. He had assumed that Hilary and Marie would follow the men in a second vehicle and that when they found the lion, the women would be left behind while the men set off to hunt their quarry on foot. Hilary was not about to be sidelined, however, and insisted that she would travel in the same vehicle as her husband, and would walk with him every step of the way. André picked up her tone and decided against trying to argue otherwise.

During the night, the temperature dropped below freezing. There was a log burner in their chalet and George refuelled it before they went to bed, and turned down the airflow so that the wood burned slowly. It was getting light at 07h00 when they got up, and they were still able to warm their hands on the log burner. André had warned that they should wear plenty of layers that they could shed as the day warmed up.

They decided to take their coffee and breakfast outside at the fire, which was blazing again, to make the most of the outdoors lifestyle. At 8h45, ready for a day of action, they left the compound and headed for the shooting range in order to sight in George's borrowed rifle before setting off lion hunting. André and George sat up front in the white, long-wheelbase Toyota bakkie (pick-up truck), and Hilary shared the rear seat with two cased rifles. On the open back of the bakkie were Pieter, looking professional and serious with his rifle pointing skywards, and two trackers.

At the range André took a USA-built bolt-action Weatherby rifle from the back seat, removed it from its case and handed it to George, together with a box of .375 bullets. Pieter and André exchanged glances as they noticed the practised and familiar way George handled the weapon. Normally they would have offered advice and given instructions, but instead all they did was set targets up at 80 and 100 metres. André had recently zeroed the rifle's sight, and when George fired three shots into each target, both groups were almost dead centre, and the holes were so close together that a five-rand coin touched all three in each target. George was slightly embarrassed by the backslapping that followed his shooting, but he was relieved as well. He was hoping he would kill his lion cleanly with a single shot; at least he now knew he could rely on his rifle.

Everyone got back into the vehicle and they headed for the gate into the 2,000-hectare hunting enclosure. There was a large notice on the gate warning that those who entered did so at their own risk. The notice backed up various forms that George and Hilary had had to sign, which absolved the PH and the farm owner of any liability in case of an accident.

Sometimes hunts were attended and observed by a representative from 'Nature Conservation' but they didn't always actually attend, although they always knew when hunts were taking place because permits had to be applied for, and granted.

As they drove slowly along a sandy track, André again took George through the details of how the hunt would happen, while Hilary listened intently. The enclosure was crisscrossed by several sandy tracks, which had been swept the afternoon before. Sweeping involved towing a dry bush behind a vehicle to wipe out as many animal tracks as possible. This was done to make lion tracks easier to spot as they drove slowly along. Pieter and the trackers hung out over the sides of the vehicle scanning the sandy surface for lion spoor, while André alternately squinted at the track in front as he drove, or examined the ground with his head out of the window.

André kept up a running commentary identifying assorted tracks, and often stopping to get out for a closer look at something that interested him. He had explained that when they found lion tracks going into a block, they would then drive around it to see if they re-emerged. If the tracks didn't re-emerge, they knew which block the lion was in, and would then return to the spoor they had first seen, climb out of the vehicle and follow the spoor on foot.

George was excited and nervous, but he also had nagging doubts flitting across the back of his mind. Two thousand hectares is nearly 5,000 acres, so they were looking in a big area. He had known from the start that he would hunt a captive-bred lion in an enclosed area, but now that he was actually close to shooting the animal, he was bothered by the fact that ultimately it couldn't escape. The method of using the sandy tracks to locate the spoor and narrow down the position of the lion was clever, but it tilted the odds further away from the lion and, given enough time, made a kill a certainty. Back in the States, these concerns had not really troubled him, but now they were coming into sharper focus with each passing minute.

Most hunters wanted to have their lion's head mounted as a trophy, and George had always thought he would do this. However, the law in the United States had changed the year before, and trophies from captive-bred lions could no longer be imported into America. What would happen to his lion's body had not been discussed, but George felt sure that André would somehow find a way to benefit from the disposal of the carcass.

They had entered the enclosure just before 9h00, and three hours later, when they stopped for coffee, snacks and a comfort break, they had still seen no lion tracks. At this point, Hilary asked George to bring a rifle and come and stand guard over her while she relieved herself behind a bush. André was not happy when Hilary walked over 50 metres into cover, having warned that it wasn't only lions they should watch out for – there were also snakes and other potential dangers. Fortunately, the guests returned safely. Having consumed and then packed up their picnic, the party was ready to resume the hunt.

It was just after 13h00 when Pieter banged gently on the roof of the vehicle, signalling André to stop. The men all got out and huddled round some fresh lion spoor running parallel to the track. George and Hilary joined the little group studying the spoor where it crossed over the track and disappeared into the bush on the other side. Pieter and one of the trackers stayed with the spoor, which had been pronounced as being very fresh, while the others got back into the vehicle. They slowly drove along the track surrounding the block, and could find no exit spoor, which meant the lion was still in this particular block.

When they got back to where they had left Pieter, he had information for them. He pointed to a large green tree: 'I followed the spoor past that tree into the grass; it is very, very fresh and I don't think he is far away. I think he is a big one and if I had to guess I would say he is under one of those trees in the dry grass.' André instructed Pieter and the trackers to lead, then George would follow, and he and Hilary would bring up the rear. They set off and George realised he knew exactly how large the lion was, and what it would look like. Hilary had chosen it from a menu of photographs on the hunting outfitter's website. His heart thudded against his ribs as he followed the trackers bent low over the spoor.

More by luck than skill, the lion had killed a warthog at daybreak. The lion had been half asleep and was largely hidden by the tall grass he was lying in, with the wind blowing his scent away from the warthog, when the unfortunate prey had all but blundered into the crouching predator. Pent-up hunger, anger, stress, uncertainty and frustration had all powered the lion's efforts in the brief struggle that followed.

Now, with a full belly and the remains of his kill nearby, the lion was dozing when he picked up the familiar sound of a vehicle's engine approaching. He had lost the captive pride he had lived with and was alone in strange surroundings. But it was with curiosity rather than alarm that he lifted his head, and looked in the direction of the noise. He saw a vehicle stop a little distance away from where he lay, but didn't move as people got out of the vehicle and walked around examining the ground. The vehicle then drove off, leaving people behind who continued examining the ground before walking in his direction. He was used to humans; they had been in his life every day since his birth. Indeed, his life had started with humans, who had bottle fed him after he had been removed from his mother. Humans were nothing to fear; in his early life they had been a source of comfort as well as food.

His instinct was almost to get up and go and greet the people that now walked towards him, but a stronger sixth sense took over and he crouched lower in the tall grass. They didn't talk as they approached and he was lying flat in the grass so that he couldn't see them, but when they stopped, turned and walked away again he was aware of it, and raised his head to watch them go. Back at the track the man with the gun lit a cigarette and both men stood waiting.

A few minutes later the vehicle returned, and more people emerged and started walking slowly towards him. Their attention was split between the ground and the bush ahead of them as they walked slowly and carefully, and every step brought them closer to where he lay.

It is a legal requirement that hunters must leave their vehicle and track their quarry on foot. This had been one of many things that had convinced George that he was going to take part in a real hunt. All of his previous worries and considerations had gone now, and he was intent only on his lion. In stress situations where danger may be involved we all wonder how we will perform, and how we will measure up to others in similar circumstances. As he slowly placed one foot in front of the other, George hoped that in André and Pieter's eyes he would compare favourably with hunters they had guided in the past.

One of the trackers had almost animal-like intuition, and seemed able to feel where the lion lay rather than needing to see it. He stopped and whispered to André and pointed. Pieter was a few paces ahead with George and the other tracker, and André hissed at him to get his attention. Now six sets of eyes, three of them aided by binoculars, scanned the grass where the man had pointed.

Although something still made him wary, the lion saw no reason to move away. When the humans stopped walking towards him, he raised his head to see what was happening. In the end, he would never have escaped, but lifting his head was a mistake that hastened his death. A fence surrounded the enclosure, preventing escape, and another fence in his mind stopped him from identifying humans as a threat. He was trapped by both physical and mental constraints.

They all saw the lion lift his head to look at them, and he continued looking at them while Pieter told George where to place his shot. He couldn't see it in detail, but from the position and angle of the head, Pieter knew exactly where the lion's shoulder was – the target for a fatal shot in the heart. George was in familiar territory and instinct took over. At just 60 metres from the

A poster at Lionsrock explains canned hunting to visitors.

lion, he was confident he could place his bullet precisely where he wanted it. He declined the offer of a prop to steady his weapon, instead wrapping the leather sling around part of his left arm, and he sighted on his lion.

The massive head sprang into focus, almost as if within touching distance. As his finger squeezed slowly on the trigger with first pressure, George relaxed and slowed his breathing, then held his breath; he didn't want anything, even the rhythm of his own breathing, to spoil the chance of a single killing shot. A fraction of a second before George reached final pressure on the trigger, the lion raised his head a little, and ever so slightly moved the front part of his body. It was enough – the .375 soft bullet, which should have crashed into the lion's heart, hit him just too low down. A massive muscular contraction and the impact of the bullet lifted the animal in a weird, grotesque backward whirl as George's second shot hammered into him. The lion now lay on its side panting and bleeding in the grass. With their guns at their shoulders, Pieter, André and George approached in single file.

George showed no emotion as, together with Hilary and the hunting team, he walked to the lion, which now lay dying with two bullets in its body. There had been none of the whoops of joy, the high fives, the congratulatory handshakes or the macho hugs that often followed the killing of a lion. The team had been ready for celebration, but as soon as George's first shot rang out his mood seemed to change.

The mortally wounded animal lay on its side and was still breathing as it looked at its killers. 'Finish him off with a shot through the eye, then it won't show when the head is mounted', said Pieter automatically as he looked down at the stricken lion.

'There's no point, it won't be mounted. You shoot it.' And with this remark, George handed his rifle to Pieter and started to move away. He hadn't gone a step before a shot rang out. He took his hat off, pushed the sunglasses up on his head, and wiped his shirt sleeve across his eyes to remove the tears he couldn't hold back. Hilary could sense her husband's mood and she walked after him.

'What is it?' she whispered. George turned and looked at his wife. 'There is only one reason that I am glad I did that: it made me realise I shouldn't have done it. I wish I hadn't.' He went back to the silent and now confused-looking hunting team still standing around the dead lion. 'I want to take the lion back with us to the lodge and burn it tonight. Its head and body are going nowhere; we will bury the remains in the morning.'

Readers must make up their own minds as to whether the killing of George's lion conforms to Safari Club International (SCI) 'fair-chase' guidelines, as followed by PHASA (see Chapter 16).

Killing his lion proved life-changing for George, and the regret would remain with him forever.

PART FOUR

Past, present and future

CHAPTER 20
HISTORY, BULLETS AND BONES

Trafalgar Square is a leading landmark in one of the world's great cities. It commemorates the British victory under Admiral Nelson over the French at the Battle of Trafalgar, and a column bearing his statue rises 52 metres above the square.

The four corners of Trafalgar Square are guarded by huge bronze lions, recumbent but with their heads up, gazing into the distance. This is just one example of how the lion is used in statuary, symbolism and architecture all over the world.

Huge bronze lions guard the corners of London's Trafalgar Square.

The 'king of the animal world' is widely called upon: 'as lazy as a lion' describes idle individuals; 'lion-hearted' is often used to indicate bravery, as in 'Richard the Lionheart'; and Emperor Haile Selassie was known as 'The Conquering Lion of the tribe of Judah'. The English, Irish, Scottish and Welsh combine and play rugby as a team known as the British Lions. In European heraldry, the lion and the unicorn are often used as symbols. In entertainment, *The Lion, The Witch and the Wardrobe* and *The Lion King* have thrilled audiences for years. Much earlier, in ancient Rome, gladiators fought lions, and professed Christians were 'thrown to the lions'. And 13 African countries use the lion as a national symbol in their coats of arms.

It is hardly surprising that the lion occupies a pre-eminent place in mythology, history, symbolism and architecture because its range once extended throughout the whole African continent, parts of southern Europe, what is now the Middle East, and much of the rest of Asia. In past centuries humans tried to use the power and magic of lions in many ways. Warriors wore lion skins into battle, and images of lions and the word 'lion' itself were used to embolden and empower.

Today, the lion is fighting its own battle for survival. Its place in history may be secure, but its future as a free-roaming species is anything but certain, now that its range and numbers have shrunk to such a degree that many question whether the king of the animal kingdom is heading for extinction in the wild.

Figures quoted by wildlife trade investigator and campaigner Karl Ammann give insight into the potential profits involved in the lion-bone trade. The figures clearly and dramatically illustrate why the lion species will now have to fight its most important battle yet to avoid becoming a relic of the past, remembered only by images, statues and tall stories.

A 15–18-kilogram lion or tiger skeleton is initially sold for $1,500–$1,800. At an average of $1,650, the 800 carcasses in the South Africa 2017 quota are collectively worth $1,320,000 before processing. When boiled, a skeleton delivers about 60 portions (bars) of tiger or lion 'cake'. Of course, there are middlemen between the first seller and the final

Oliver Peirce-Gregory

The king of the animal world is widely portrayed in daily life.

Wildlife traffic investigator Karl Ammann inspects a pair of elephant tusks.

consumer: the processor, wholesaler and retailer all have profit margins and, in many cases, smugglers and others will have taken their cuts too. Each bar sells for $1,000, so each skeleton is worth $60,000 by the time it has been processed and sold to the end consumer as 'tiger' cake. By now the 800 skeletons will collectively be worth a staggering $48,000,000!

Before 2007 the export of live lions and lion parts was an 'unremarkable blip' in global wildlife trade, according to a report by TRAFFIC. The South African lion-bone trade surged in 2007 soon after the hunting of captive-bred lions became increasingly popular, and from 2014 to 2016 South Africa legally exported an estimated 1,300 lion skeletons each year.

It is well known in the wildlife trade sector that the surge in interest and value of lion bones is due to a shortage of tiger products, for which there is an ever-increasing demand. It is almost impossible to tell the difference between tiger and lion carcasses, which is why lion bones are now being substituted and sold as tiger products – a trick about which the South African government cannot fail to be aware.

In addition to the marketing of carcasses for body parts, it is only relatively recently that lions have become such a commercial species in other ways too: cub petting, 'voluntourism', walking with lions, hunting captive-bred animals, and the bone trade are all profit opportunities that didn't exist 30 years ago. Before this, lions were only of commercial value in zoos, safari parks, eco-tourism, in films and advertising, and to 'real' trophy hunters.

In Southeast Asia, lion products are mainly sold as tiger, and the list of products is growing all the time. Tiger cake, tiger wine, skins, skulls, claws, teeth and tails are all being used for medicinal or decorative (jewellery) purposes. As with rhino horn, lion products are making the 'health-to-wealth' transition, and are increasingly being bought as much for status reasons as for their supposed health benefits. In China and Vietnam, being able to offer guests tiger wine or tiger cake, or wearing tiger jewellery, are all serious status symbols, and the dealers are constantly creating new products. Karl Ammann has come across skulls being sold for $16,000 and skins for $6,000. To have a bottle of tiger 'wine' with a penis and testicles floating in it is the king of status symbols, and Ammann has a record of just a penis being sold for $2,500. He says that claws can be worth up to $500 apiece, and large canine teeth can be worth thousands. Before being sold, lion skins have plastic canines substituted for the real teeth because the originals are so valuable.

Ammann and others are critical of South Africa for leading the way in commercialising and commodifying a wild species. Ammann put it succinctly: 'For the sake of profits they [South Africa] are taking the "wild" out of wildlife, the "wild" out of wilderness, and are helping a bunch of crooks to get richer'.

Lion taxidermy trophies, whether involving just the head or the whole body, generally use only the skin wrapped over a wire armature to fill out the body shape and re-create a lifelike animal. Skeletons are therefore a by-product of the process that can go straight into the lion-bone trade and, depending on how much of the lion is preserved, there will also be other body parts for sale. While the taxidermy trade is one

A lion skeleton

loophole allowing dealers and traders to beat international laws and regulations, another is 'in-country' processing. Once a skeleton has been made into 'cake bars' it is no longer obviously identifiable as a lion or tiger product, which makes it easier to move over borders whether legally or illegally.

Ammann has heard reports of hunters in Tanzania and Zimbabwe being approached by dealers' representatives offering to buy lion products. He is also aware of two Vietnamese nationals who have set up lion- and tiger-processing facilities in South Africa, buying carcasses and producing finished products.

Vietnam and China are the main consumer markets. Other countries like Cambodia and Thailand are smaller consumers, and Laos is the main entry port, with the size of the market in each country heavily influenced by the size of its local Chinese and Vietnamese populations. In Vietnam, all tiger (lion) products are popular, but in China it is mostly tiger wine that is in demand.

According to the CITES trade database, Laos has a dominant position in the bone trade. Between 2009 and 2015 Laos bought over 2,000 complete skeletons from South Africa, and this figure excludes 2,300 bones and 40 skulls bought separately in the same period and sold as 'incomplete skeletons'.

To make tiger wine and other products, large aquarium fish tanks about two metres long are filled with alcohol in which skeletons are placed. In Vietnam, where tiger glue or cake are the popular products, skeletons are boiled in water, often with products from other animals, such as muntjac (a small Chinese deer) bones and turtle shell, added. The process used to take several days but the use of pressure cookers has speeded this up. The gravy-like residue that floats on top is scooped off to make the 'cake' bars. Products from this process are often added to ordinary wine, which

China, Vietnam and other Far Eastern countries are the markets for lion products that are often passed off as being derived from tigers.

is then sold as tiger wine, and ginseng is a popular addition to the mix. In China, tiger wine tanks commonly have a little tap on them to allow customers to serve themselves straight from the tank.

In China and Laos well-heeled consumers go to tiger farms to select their animal. It is then killed, usually by electrocution, and the buyer chooses which body parts they want processed. The starting price will be based on the whole carcass weight, which will probably be about 200 kilograms, from which 8 kilograms is deducted for the intestines, which have no value. The farm will then buy back unwanted parts, which means that consumers will eventually pay only for the body parts they have chosen.

Laos is not just a major importer of lion products, it is also where many commercial tiger farms are located, although the government committed last year to closing down the farms. The majority of tiger farms, however, are in China, where there are probably 5,000–6,000 tigers at about 100 breeding facilities – although these don't begin to meet the consumer demand.

Given the rise in middle-class wealth in Southeast Asia, and particularly in China, it is difficult to see how the market for dead lions can do anything other than continue to expand. As with rhinos (for their horns) and elephants (for ivory), lions are now a valuable trading commodity.

The UN body set up to monitor and control the trade in endangered species is the Convention on International Trade in Endangered Species of Wild Fauna and Flora (CITES). Drafted in 1963 following a resolution adopted at a meeting of the International Union for the Conservation of Nature (IUCN), the text of the resolution was finally accepted in Washington in March 1973 by 80 countries, and on 1 July 1975, the Convention came into force. CITES is an international agreement to which countries voluntarily subscribe, and its provisions are supposed to be binding on member states, which are known as Parties. CITES provisions do not take the place of national laws, but each Party has to ensure that its domestic legislation reflects Convention text and resolutions and has to implement them.

CITES is often wrongly thought of as a conservation organisation. This is not the case – rather it is 'an international agreement between governments, its aim is to ensure that international trade in specimens of wild animals and plants does not threaten their survival' (CITES website).

CITES has its headquarters in Geneva, and in April 2016 there were 183 signatories (Parties) to the Convention. Every two to three years there is a Conference of the Parties (COP), and threatened flora and fauna species are proposed for listing to regulate or stop international trade in them. Levels of trade are regulated and defined by listing on one of three appendices: Appendix I, II or III. Appendix I is for the most endangered animals and plants, which are threatened by international trade. All commercial trade is prohibited and trade in Appendix I species can only be for scientific research or in special circumstances. Appendix II allows specific controlled international commercial trade that is monitored by CITES and controlled by a permitting system to ensure that the trade does not prove detrimental to the survival of the listed species in the wild. Appendix III is a list of species included at the request of a Party that already regulates trade in the species, but that needs the help and co-operation of other Parties to prevent unsustainable or illegal exploitation of the species.

In recent years lion populations have been declining for many reasons, and there is no doubt that their increased commodity value is one of the things putting pressure on the species. The last CITES COP was held in Johannesburg in September/October 2016. At this conference, African lions were proposed for an Appendix I listing, which did not succeed. Although trade is regulated under Appendix II, licensed trophy hunting is still allowed, and at COP 17 South Africa was granted a special dispensation allowing its captive-lion breeders to continue to trade in bones. CITES failed to stipulate any criteria to guide this decision, which meant the South African authorities could pick any number they chose and simply inform CITES of it. In June 2017 South Africa proposed an annual carcass quota of 800 skeletons. The figure of 800 seems to have been based on data contained in the South African National Biodiversity Institute (SANBI) study of January 2017. This report suggested that a harvest of 800 lions per year from the captive breeding population was sustainable based on past trophy-hunting numbers and carcass exports.

Although the trade exemption applies only to captive-bred lions, and so at first sight should not impact negatively on wild populations, conservationists and lion ecologists are adamant that captive breeding, and the trade that it supplies, will impact negatively on wild populations for the following reasons:

- In any commodity, an increase in supply results in an increase in demand.
- A legal trade provides opportunities to launder illegally sourced products.
- Saying that any trade is allowed sends a very dangerous message, because consumers are often unaware of the difference between captive-bred and wild animals – to them, a lion is a lion.
- If trade is allowed and is seen to be profitable, it is almost certain that other countries will start large-scale captive-lion breeding programmes and apply for the same exemption already granted to South Africa. There are already reports of captive-lion breeding farms being set up in Zimbabwe, Zambia and Namibia.

Profit opportunities will be exploited whether legal or illegal.
The eyes that look back at us from trafficked humans and
factory-farmed animals should make us all feel guilty.

CHAPTER 21

CONSERVATION AND THE WAY FORWARD

According to the IUCN Red List, African lion populations declined by 43 per cent between 1993 and 2014. Lions now occupy only about 8 per cent of their original historic range area. In Africa in recent decades they have disappeared from between 12 and 16 of their original range states. The only countries with significant populations are Botswana, South Africa, Zimbabwe, Tanzania and Kenya. Lions still exist in several other countries but in small numbers. Of particular concern is West Africa, where it is thought that only about 400 individuals remain. In West, Central and East Africa the aggregated decline is roughly 60 per cent in the last 21 years.

In the years leading up to CITES COP 17, held in 2016 in Johannesburg, an IUCN group led by Dr Hans Bauer did a study of Africa's lion populations. Their work concluded that there were some 20,000–30,000 lions left living wild on the continent, and they made it clear that they had more confidence in the lower figure of 20,000. Independent work carried out by a British-based NGO called LionAid puts the figure even lower, at just 13,000–15,000.

The lower figures quoted by LionAid are backed up by recent (July 2017) reports funded by the Panthera Foundation, which indicated that in southeast Angola only 10–30 lions were found. According to LionAid, this contrasted with a previous IUCN report in 2006, which estimated 750–1,000 lions in that area, and called Angola a 'lion stronghold'. Also in 2006, Senegal was quoted as having around 1,600 lions, and subsequent surveys reduced this number to as low as 16. Some southern African populations are holding their own or even increasing, but the general trend is one of alarming decline.

Despite their size and their fearsome reputation as apex predators, lions are actually quite a fragile species and are susceptible to a range of anthropogenic or human-induced factors.

The 'Man Eaters of Tsavo' once terrorised a part of Kenya when they started attacking and eating people building a railway. This unusual lion behaviour took place in 1898, possibly as a result of reduced natural prey species from a rinderpest outbreak. Only two lions were involved, and they were hunted down and shot amidst much publicity – and possibly exaggerated claims about the number of victims. In those days humans often had cause to fear lions, but for the last few decades ever-increasing human populations have meant that lions have much more reason to fear us than we have to fear them.

In the previous chapter, we looked at the recent rise in the value of lion body parts due to increasing demand from Southeast Asia, where lion products are passed off as tiger – a demand that is fuelled and supplied largely by the South African captive-breeding industry. However, it also impacts on wild populations and this relatively new demand is only one of many factors that are contributing to the decline in lion numbers. Some of the many other factors are listed below, not necessarily in order of importance.

Habitat loss

In some parts of Africa aridity and desertification have led to reduced water resources and caused declines in prey species numbers. However, the main habitat loss factor is human encroachment. Increasing human populations require more land as they expand into areas that were once wilderness, leading to loss of the original flora and fauna, including the prey species that lived on it.

Human-Wildlife Conflict (HWC)

Once prey species have been replaced by domestic animals like cattle, sheep and goats, lions and other predators will often turn to this new food source. Rural Africans and nomadic herding tribes have coexisted with wildlife for centuries, but as human populations have increased, with more nomads and larger herds living on less land, more efficient means of killing 'nuisance' predators have been developed. The natural balances that existed have largely been lost as available space has dwindled.

Prey-base decline

Although a separate issue, prey-base decline is inextricably linked to HWC as discussed above.

Hunting and trophy hunting

The excessive killing of wild African species in the 19th and 20th centuries, mostly by European and American 'sportsmen', was a huge factor in reducing their populations. The trophy hunting of lions mostly involved large males with big manes. Females and smaller males were also often shot, but it was, and is, the big, maned males that are most sought after.

It was thought that shooting single males in prides had little effect on the pride and on lion numbers. Many experts, including conservationist Derek Joubert, lion expert Dr Pieter Kat and others believe that killing large males has contributed significantly to the decline in lion numbers. When a pride male is killed and another male takes over his role, the newcomer generally kills all his predecessor's cubs – a brutal version of not wanting to bring up someone else's children, and of limiting their genetic legacy. It also brings the females in the pride quickly back into oestrus, and ready to breed again. Breeding is not the only thing affected when a senior male is killed – there is also the loss of acquired knowledge and experience, and the stability of the whole pride structure is thrown out of balance.

Disease

Feline AIDS, Bovine Tuberculosis (BTB), canine distemper and other diseases have all contributed to lion population losses. LionAid cites the example of one outbreak of canine distemper in 1994 that wiped out 1,000 of an estimated population of 3,000 lions in the Serengeti in Tanzania.

Poaching

An increase in demand almost always leads to increases in price and supply; this is also true of lion body parts. Some argue that a legal supply, such as the 800 South African carcasses, will reduce illegal supply and poaching. Past evidence with other species in similar circumstances points to the opposite being true, and most experts believe that the South African breeding industry will eventually result in an increase in poaching of wild lions.

All the factors that have contributed to lion population reduction are related. This means that the decline can be reversed only by taking a range of actions that are also connected. Some experts and conservationists believe that a complete cessation of all lion hunting would allow populations to stabilise, buying time for other co-ordinated measures. This would require only the main hunting-range states of Zimbabwe, Namibia, Tanzania and Zambia to put a ban in place. In Botswana hunting has already been banned, and in South Africa very few wild permits are issued, and most 'hunted' lions come from the captive-bred population.

Current population estimates vary between LionAid's 13,000 at the low end, to 30,000 at the top end of the IUCN research. Clearly, a plan can't be formulated without an accurate comprehensive numerical survey of Africa's remaining wild lions. Wildlife philanthropist Paul Allen recently invested close to $10 million for a 'continent-wide' count of Africa's elephants. If a similar exercise were carried out for lions, scientists and conservationists would be able to plan much more effectively.

Properly managed and administered national park areas can mitigate many of the related factors such as Human-Wildlife Conflict, human encroachment, prey-base reduction, and poaching. Wildlife is one of Africa's most valuable assets, and an ever-increasing global human population means that ever more tourists will pay to come and view the animals. Figures have often shown that, when run efficiently, national parks can make significant profits, supporting the view that 'if it pays it stays'.

The Born Free Foundation and others run programmes in many places aimed at limiting HWC and promoting habitat enhancement. At the time of writing (July 2017), the Convention on Migratory Species (CMS) is planning to discuss an African Carnivore Initiative at a Conference of Parties in October 2017. CMS may seek to develop an over-arching initiative to facilitate the development of regional collaborative conservation programmes. These could involve lions, wild dogs, leopards, cheetahs and possibly hyenas. With the exceptions of Botswana and Namibia, most of the main lion range states are signatories to CMS, and Botswana is considering joining. A CMS (as opposed to CITES) Appendix II listing for lions would mandate and empower CMS to encourage and promote the initiative among member states. This would enable a holistic approach to be taken, including the establishment of more 'linked' parks and reserves.

There are no magic-wand, one-size-fits-all solutions to stabilising and increasing lion populations because, while attrition factors are often connected, different approaches will be taken in different places. The only 'silver bullet' would be an immediate hunting ban.

Lions are good breeders, and many argue that breeding them in captivity for hunting, and their body parts, will relieve pressure on wild populations. Breeders also believe that captive-bred lions can, relatively easily, be reintroduced to the wild. This view is strongly contested by scientists and conservationists, and at the World Conservation Congress in Hawaii in 2016 the IUCN called on South Africa to close down its predator-breeding industry.

In July 2017, SAPA released information claiming that a captive-bred male and female, after having been released in December 2016 in an enclosed reserve, had produced a litter of three cubs and were successfully hunting to sustain themselves. Clear video footage backed up the SAPA information release. SAPA believes this proves that captive-bred animals can successfully transfer to the wild, and a SAPA executive council member was quoted as follows:

'It didn't come as a surprise,' said Tienie Bamberger. 'We, who have knowledge about lions in the wild and also working with lions in captive facilities, always knew that a lion retains its instincts, whether it has been born in the wild in Selous Game Reserve in Tanzania, or on a farm in the Free State. But we are still very excited to have it confirmed in a controlled and monitored programme.

'Of course this wasn't enough,' said Bamberger. 'They, these anti-hunters, then came up with the idea that these lions won't be considered wild if they do not breed successfully in the wild. Well, we knew it was just going to be a matter of time. Even we were surprised by how quickly they mated, had cubs and are raising them successfully.'

SAPA executive council member

Given the perilous state of lion populations and the adverse public opinion, it would clearly be a game changer for breeders like SAPA if a real proven conservation value were acknowledged.

Dr Mark Jones of the Born Free Foundation was less than convinced that anything of value had been proven:

'The claim that a pair of captive-bred lions released into what is presumably a fenced area may be able to hunt for themselves and rear a litter of cubs is not altogether surprising. However, it does not in any way imply that the intensive captive-breeding industry has any current or potential future role in wild lion conservation. This fact is acknowledged by the South African Government and the international scientific community (IUCN). Captive-bred lions are habituated to the presence of people, and if released may pose a significantly greater threat than their wild counterparts to the safety of people and livestock by virtue of their lack of fear of humans and human-populated areas. In addition, as well as potentially struggling to survive and thrive in the presence of truly wild lions, they might pose a risk to the genetic integrity and health of extant wild lion populations. The introduction of captive-bred animals into wild areas for conservation purposes is an

Dr Mark Jones of Born Free Foundation

Born Free Foundation

extremely complex science, the instances where this has been successfully achieved for big cats are virtually non-existent, and there is nothing that suggests South Africa's predator breeders are capable of meeting the exacting requirements of such programmes.'

Dr Mark Jones, Born Free Foundation

Conservationist and *Blood Lions* producer Pippa Hankinson commented: *'SAPA's press release states that a pair of captive lions have bred and are hunting in a programme which is "controlled and monitored" on a "reserve", but fails to mention the name of the reserve or whether a lion ecologist manages the programme.*

'As this information has not been provided I have to assume that the project has not been scientifically monitored, and that the release area is probably not part of a completely natural habitat. If this is indeed the case, then I suggest this programme does not irrefutably prove that captive-bred lions can successfully adapt when released into the wild. I believe that for a programme such as this to be acceptable to the formal scientific and conservation communities, it must be conducted under strict scientific protocols.

'Furthermore, I would point out that these lions have been captive bred and reared on a lion breeding farm, so the mother would not have the necessary skills to teach her cubs how to survive in the wild, nor would she have the capacity to integrate them into a wild lion pride. Due to this I have to doubt their ability to defend themselves in a natural, fully wild setting, particularly when pitted against wild predators.

'In conclusion, I cannot understand SAPA's reasons for going to such lengths to try and re-wild captive-bred lions when we know from internationally recognised specialist big-cat conservation organisations, such as Panthera, that captive-bred lions have no conservation value. Panthera's Dr Balme says that "the reintroduction of these genetically impaired, inbred animals would compromise the genetic integrity of wild lion populations", and that South Africa's wild lion populations are stable, so "the use of captive-bred lions as a source for repopulating or supplementing wild populations is not a viable conservation option".'

Pippa Hankinson

Vested interests will always influence views and opinions. There are lion breeders operating at various levels in different types of establishments, and many genuinely believe that there is a potential conservation value to what they are doing. However, the overwhelming weight of expert opinion from scientists, conservationists and from practical evidence indicates that captive-bred lions have no conservation value.

Africa is blessed with being home to many of the world's most recognised animal species. Together with elephants, lions are at the top of the icon tree. They are among the most awesome animals on the planet, and for their human neighbours this means a heavy responsibility. Somehow humans have to learn to live with lions as neighbours with equal rights. If this doesn't happen, lions will probably only exist in the future in museums, parks, movies and picture books.

*Lions may one day exist only in parks, movies, books
and as stuffed specimens in museum exhibits.*

EPILOGUE

A couple of months after I had put my pen down on this book I went to see Obi and Oliver again. My visit was almost an exact rerun of the last time I had met them. Obi stayed on the roof of their shelter, ignoring me while staring into the distance. Oliver flopped lazily down and padded over to meet me where the path joins the fence of their enclosure. I went and sat in the same place I had before, nearly 12 months earlier. He first sat, then lay alongside the fence looking at me in exactly the same way as before. His gaze was curious, warm and friendly; and this time I didn't find his stare threatening or worrying, and I returned it, looking straight into his eyes.

'Hello Oliver. You are looking well, and Obi is still staring into space trying to work it all out. You should tell him not to bother because it's not a pretty picture out there. You guys should live for today, and every day give thanks for where you are in a safe, secure and permanent home. I have seen hundreds of lions since we last met – very few of them looked happy, and even fewer had safe futures.

'I don't know how long people will go on breeding lions in captivity, but I do know that what I have seen is terribly wrong. I promise you I will do all I can to put a stop to the abuse. On my journey of discovery, I haven't found too many very bad people; rather, I have found people who don't understand, who think that it's okay to profit from using animals as they wish.

'You and I know this is not fair and shouldn't be happening, but I am afraid, my friend, that the world is full of what's not fair and shouldn't be happening. You must be patient, and give us time; we will stop this disgusting exploitation of your species; that is my promise to you.'

Oliver continued staring at me and of course he hadn't understood a word, but I hope that maybe by some mysterious telepathy he recognised that I am on his side. If he did, I would like to believe he might have said, 'Thank you for trying to help. I hope humans will eventually leave us alone to live our wild lives'.

STOP PRESS

The situation with regard to captive-lion breeding, and the many related issues, including trophy hunting, the sale of carcasses, captive-bred hunts, etc., is constantly changing, developing and evolving. Below is a chronological list of events that occurred between finishing writing this book and going to press. I hope this helps keep the reader as informed as possible.

July 2017 – The US lifts the ban on trophy imports from Zimbabwe.

July 2017 – Cecil the lion's son, Xanda, is shot by a trophy hunter in Zimbabwe.

July 2017 – The Environment Investigation Agency (EIA) report confirms that a ban on tiger imports by China has resulted in traders turning to lion parts from South Africa.

Aug 2017 – The Southern African Tourism Services Association annual conference looks at ways to ensure that its members book tour groups only to ethical sanctuaries, and avoid canned hunting operators.

Sept 2017 – A touring Welsh rugby player is bitten when he sticks his hand into an enclosure to stroke a lion.

Oct 2017 – A Wits University academic publishes a report indicating that over 6,000 lion skeletons had been exported from South Africa to the Asian market in the previous 10 years, the main source of skeletons being the canned lion hunting industry.

Nov 2017 – The South African Predators Association (SAPA) sends a letter to the US Administration requesting that the ban on the importation of trophies from hunting be lifted.

Nov 2017 – US President Donald Trump moves to lift the ban on the importation of lion trophies into the US, then later bows to the public backlash and puts the decision on hold pending his reviewing further evidence.

Nov 2017 – PHASA members vote at their annual AGM to follow SAPA in supporting captive-bred lion hunting, thus reversing their previous opposition (* see report on page 182).

Nov 2017 – A lion escapes from the back of a trailer in Tzaneen, South Africa.

Nov 2017 – The African Lion Conservation Community responds to the SAPA letter to US authorities (referred to above) by highlighting false statements and unsubstantiated facts contained in the letter.

THE PROFESSIONAL HUNTERS' ASSOCIATION OF SOUTH AFRICA
At its 2015 AGM a majority of members voted that the association should distance itself from captive-bred lion hunting. In November 2017 this decision was reversed when PHASA members 'accepted the responsible hunting of ranched lions on SAPA-accredited hunting ranches within the relevant legal framework and/or according to recommendations of the applicable hunting association, such as SCI fair-chase standards'.

The decision caused a split within PHASA and the resignations of members and executives followed. Many then questioned whether the association would continue to exist in its present form. As well as causing divisions within PHASA, the decision attracted widespread condemnation from hunting organisations and activists alike, as shown by the comments below.

THE OPERATORS AND PROFESSIONAL HUNTERS' ASSOCIATIONS OF AFRICA issued a media release: 'The Operators and Professional Hunters' Associations of Africa are deeply troubled by the decision made by PHASA at their AGM on November 22, 2017, to adopt a new constitution that accepts the practice of captive-bred lion hunting. The practice of captive-bred lion hunting inevitably brings the entire African hunting industry, in every African nation where hunting is permitted, into ill repute.
'PHASA's actions completely disregard one of the fundamental concepts of hunting, namely fair chase, and will, without doubt, jeopardise not only conservation efforts, but also the livelihoods of those who rely on well-managed and ethical hunting practices, far beyond the borders of South Africa. As a result, the majority of OPHAA members have decided to indefinitely suspend PHASA's membership in OPHAA until further review.'

THE WILD SHEEP FOUNDATION and hunting agency BookYourHunt.com immediately withdrew future support for PHASA: 'In the light of the recent acceptance of the shooting of captive-bred lions as a legitimate form of hunting by PHASA, we, as a concerned group of professional hunters, distance ourselves completely from such acceptance and no longer view PHASA as the legitimate mouthpiece for professional hunting in South Africa.
'A new association will be formed in the very near future and will once again reflect the traditions of responsible, ethical and conservation-based hunting in South Africa.'

THE NAMIBIA PROFESSIONAL HUNTERS' ASSOCIATION echoed their colleagues' sentiments: 'The approval of this motion flies in the face of all that is deemed to be ethical hunting by the overwhelming majority of hunting associations in Africa and around the world.'

This update was compiled in December 2017 and doubtless debate over this issue will continue. During December a new body called 'The Custodians of Professional Hunting and Conservation South Africa (CPHCSA) was formed and past PHASA President Stewart Dorrington was elected as the chair of the new organisation.

January 23 2018 – The South African Government Department of Environmental Affairs published a document detailing their non-detriment findings with regard to South Africa's three lion populations – wild, managed wild, and captive. Wildlife conservation and animal welfare NGOs were disappointed with, and critical of, the document.

27 February 2018 – A young woman was mauled to death by a lioness at 'lion whisperer' Kevin Richardson's wildlife sanctuary. The tragedy has re-ignited debate on all forms of so called 'lion eco-tourism'.

I promise you I will do all I can to put a stop to the abuse.

THE OFFICIAL STANDPOINT

Blood Lions

Ian Michler – Blood Lions team

I hadn't wanted to believe that sentient wild animals, which normally live in highly structured family groups (prides), were being factory farmed like domestic livestock. Obi and Oliver's story and *Blood Lions* had prepared us for what we would find and, to an extent, preconditioned our opinions. Nevertheless, I suppose we were hoping it wouldn't be as bad as we had been led to believe. It turned out to be worse.

Our journey of discovery clearly showed that captive-lion breeding is happening on a larger scale than we had expected. We had wondered whether a campaigning film, and the two passionate and driven women who had rescued Obi and Oliver, might have overstated or overdramatised the story. We discovered the reverse to be true, and I came to the conclusion that, unless and until public attitudes and the government's position change, captive-lion breeding will continue.

I tried hard to get a meeting with Thea Carrol of the Department of Environmental Affairs, but this proved impossible, so the DEA kindly agreed that I could send in a list of questions instead.

After receiving the DEA's answers, I asked for comments on them from the *Blood Lions* team, Gareth Patterson, Four Paws and The Campaign Against Canned Hunting (CACH). What follows are questions in bold text, followed by the DEA's answers, along with embedded comments giving an up-to-date picture (mid-2017) of the positions of the two sides in the debate.

TO : Richard Peirce
FROM : RPA Consult
EMAIL : rpaconsult@peirceshark.com
TIME-FRAME : 15 MARCH 2017
RE : KISS ME, CUDDLE ME BOOK INPUTS

QUESTIONS:

1. CITES decision 14:69 prohibits the breeding of tigers for the supply of body parts for commercial trade because everyone accepted that this would stimulate the poaching of wild tigers. The position of your department varies from this i.e. you seem to be saying it is different for lions, why do you say this?

[DEA's response]

The position varies because there is no evidence that the breeding of lion in captivity has a negative impact on the survival of the species in the wild. In fact, a study conducted by TRAFFIC and released in 2015, titled: 'Bones of Contention: An assessment of the South African trade in African Lion Panthera leo bones and other body parts' found that in South Africa, the trade in lion bones currently has a negligible impact on wild lion populations. The South African government will continue to monitor this situation.

Ian Michler – Blood Lions team

The DEA answer is extremely short-sighted as the TRAFFIC report covers a relatively short period and most of this was before the significant increase in lion bone trade had occurred. Are they suggesting they have not learnt anything from the tiger bone, abalone or ivory trade sagas and that they will wait until wild lion populations are being heavily impacted? We would also draw their attention to the assessment of SANBI. 'The trade in P. leo bones for Traditional Medicine (in Africa as well as Asia) has been identified as an emerging threat to the species (Bauer et al, 2015)'. https://cites.org/sites/default/files/eng/cop/17/InfDocs/E-CoP17-Inf-78.pdf

And the African Lion Working Group has also warned against allowing a trade in lion bone. DEA has taken a reckless approach with financial considerations being their primary criteria at the moment.

Fiona Miles — Director, Four Paws South Africa
At the CITES Conference held in Johannesburg in 2016 one of [the] key points that was agreed upon is that South Africa needs a comprehensive independent study to be conducted around its lion population, addressing wild, population controlled and captive lions. This study would allow all parties to input their evidence and from that we would be able to derive a collective consensus and only then can we determine impact. To date the DEA has not moved on implementing this study.

We can start a long process of quoting various studies, and by the DEA cherry picking this one, they are disregarding others that have had less variable outcomes.

The need for a comprehensive independent study is clear.

2. There is media-published anecdotal evidence from Botswana that wild lion prides are being attacked at the instigation of SA lion farmers in order to capture cubs to introduce fresh blood to their breeding stocks. Is the DEA aware of this, and if so what are you doing about it?

[DEA's response]
The DEA is aware of sporadic cases over the years where lion cubs were illegally captured and brought across the border into South Africa (into the Northern Cape and North West provinces) from Botswana. We do not however have evidence that this is happening on the scale alluded to in the question and would encourage that if the media has concrete evidence of these attacks and those involved that this should be provided to our Enforcement unit for further investigation together with the Directorate for Priority Crime Investigation (DPCI).

It should further be noted that interventions have been put in place by the DEA together with the provincial environmental/conservation authorities to train border officials in order to detect and curb wildlife trafficking through ports of entry and exit. Engagements with the Botswana authorities are also ongoing and during the previous SA-Botswana Bi-National Commission held in South Africa in November 2016, it was noted that the two countries continue to undertake coordinated border patrols, intelligence and information sharing to combat poaching and illegal wildlife trade.

Monitoring measures have also been put in place within South Africa to ensure that compliance monitoring is undertaken on a regular basis at lion breeding facilities and a condition of the permit for lion breeders requires that they keep a stud book to record all the lions in their possession, including offspring and to submit such a stud book monthly to provincial authorities. The inspections of these facilities have also been elevated to a national project, thus ensuring a co-ordinated effort to monitor this sector between DEA and the affected provinces. During 2016/17, this project was rolled out in Limpopo and parts of the Free State province and in 2017/18 the remainder of the Free State will be covered together with the North West province.

Ian Michler — Blood Lions team

From my understanding and research, the DEA answer is mostly correct. There is little to no evidence that this is still taking place on a scale other than sporadic incidents of opportunism.

Fiona Miles — Director, Four Paws South Africa

The DEA confirms that they are aware of sporadic incidents but the truth is that this is more widespread and not only from just outside of our borders but also within, as farmers work towards introducing new genetic material. The truth is that years of inbreeding within the canned lion hunting industry has created weak genetic lions with deformities. The Johannesburg Zoo currently has a prime example of this with a white lion that they are caring for who through inbreeding has a severe spine deformity.

We are clearly all in agreement that this is happening and sporadic reported cases leads to the question, how many cases are not being [reported]. Also, we cannot discount the fact that cross border smuggling and the accompanying incidents of bribery and officials 'looking the other way' is a reality in South Africa. As much as the DEA says they are monitoring the situation we must ask how are they doing this monitoring and what measures have really been actively put in place? What concrete results are there to show right now in terms of enforcement?

3. The IUCN passed motion 009 at its conference in Hawaii in 2016 and called on the SA government to phase out lion farming and captive-lion trophy hunting. Does the DEA understand why this ban was requested?

[DEA's response]

Yes, in so far as IUCN members have rights to raise their views and positions for consideration in IUCN conferences.

Ian Michler – Blood Lions team

The political response is correct in that the IUCN has no mandate to force changes with regard to the laws within member states. These have to be done through amendments to Acts in Parliament. But government is also saying that South Africa is thumbing its nose at the decision taken by the overwhelming majority of IUCN members and, despite their commitment to review the request to close down the captive breeding industry, they will not bother to engage on the issue. Again, from my understanding this has little to do with conservation objectives – instead it is driven by a lobby that serves the financial benefits to farmers and others involved, both directly and indirectly, in the predator breeding industry.

Fiona Miles – Director, Four Paws South Africa

The motion clearly carried very little weight with the DEA and they are moving in the exact opposite direction by introducing a quota. This is extremely concerning as we are clearly moving against international sentiment that is in place for very specific reasons. We also need to ask the question why the DEA is placing so little weight behind this motion. Why is international sentiment being ignored and the reputation risk to South Africa being allowed to increase?

4. If yes to the above question, why has the DEA ignored the request?

[DEA's response]

The Department of Environmental Affairs explained to the proponents of the motion that certain requirements contained in the motion cannot be implemented due to legal implications. For example: The government cannot prohibit an activity on the basis of the IUCN motion. The Minister of Environmental Affairs is legally mandated by an act of Parliament, particularly the National Environmental Management: Biodiversity Act, 2004 (Act No 10 of 2004), to prohibit an activity/ activities that have a negative impact on the survival of the species in the wild. As mentioned above, the captive breeding of lion and the trade in bones were not found to be threatening to the survival of the species in the wild.

Ian Michler – Blood Lions team

We refer the DEA to the statement from Panthera, one of the world's leading predator conservation agencies:

'Proponents of the captive lion trade argue the industry reduces demand for wild lion parts, thereby benefitting wild lion conservation. However, there is significant evidence that South Africa's legal trade in captive-bred lion trophies is accelerating the slaughter of wild lions for their parts in neighbouring countries and is in fact increasing demand for wild lion parts in Asia – a market that did not exist before South Africa started exporting lion bones in 2007.' https://www.panthera.org/cms/sites/default/files/Panthera_PressRelease_LionBones.pdf

Ignoring input of the IUCN and the leading predator conservation experts is an extremely irresponsible stance from the DEA.

Fiona Miles – Director, Four Paws South Africa
Again, this is linked to the utilisation of very specific studies that provide the outcomes that the DEA finds convenient. As mentioned earlier we have and continue to call for a comprehensive independent study commissioned by the DEA that will look at all aspects around the lion populations (both wild and captive) and movement in South Africa. This needs to be done in a transparent and open fashion that will allow all parties to input and provide the relevant evidence they have.

The DEA also does not tell us what they see as forming part of the wild lion population. Are they using only truly wild lions in open reserves or are they including lions in controlled population environments? Also, do they include any figures from captive lions in stating that the wild animal population is not affected?

What has not been touched on is animal welfare and the appalling conditions that many of the canned lions are being kept in and the ethical question around the 'farming' of a wild animal for economic gain as is being done by the canned lion industry.

5. Why did the DEA actually respond by saying it would not follow the IUCN's request and close down lion breeding facilities?

(DEA's response)
See the response above.

Fiona Miles – Director, Four Paws South Africa
The mere fact that an industry may or may not be affecting the wild population does not

address the ethical side of whether an industry should be permitted to exist. If we take all the figures out of the equation, do we ethically as a country want to be involved in this practice? We sincerely hope that the answer is no.

6. Does the DEA believe that lion farming gives employment?

[DEA's response]
Based on a study conducted by the Department in 2009 through the University of Free State, lion farms do provide employment.

Ian Michler — Blood Lions team
The employment argument is overplayed and also needs to be contextualised. The lion industry contributes less than a fraction of 1 per cent to the overall tourism turnover figures. In addition, of the more than 9 million annual foreign visitors to South Africa, less than 1,000 come to kill lions in captivity. Furthermore, most of the breeders are farmers that have simply shifted from producing agricultural products to breeding lions. Their workforce remains similar in size, but their job descriptions change slightly.
And lastly, the government needs to investigate the number of jobs the 'voluntourism' industry is actually taking away from South Africans. Some of these lion facilities have in excess of 30 volunteers paying to work: they are taking away paid jobs that could go to South Africans.

Fiona Miles — Director, Four Paws South Africa
The employment provided by a lion farm compared to other industries is minimal. The economic impact is also very limited as canned lion hunters travel to the country for a few days at a time. Traditional hunting safaris for instance had visitors remain in the country for weeks (21 days on average) as they must track animals over vast areas. The accommodation and catering costs, incidental costs and the hiring of trackers and guides was substantially more than the current figures.

The economic impact of canned lion hunting is limited to a few choice individuals who find it extremely lucrative and we are seeing our natural resource, heritage and people exploited for the advancement of a select group.

7. The DEA must be aware that rural employment has reduced from 1.6 million to 650,000 and at the same time the number of farms turning over from agriculture to game breeding has increased and now exceeds 10,000. So, at the time that game breeding has been increasing, rural employment has been decreasing. Your comments please, because on the basis of these figures, lion farming is actually causing unemployment, having taken over from previous agricultural uses.

(DEA's response)
There seems to be an assumption that rural employment is only provided by agriculture and 'game breeding'. Rural development and employment is a more complex matter; and it's therefore an incorrect statement made by the author. The author is advised to undertake more work in terms of rural development and the dynamics relating to it, to avoid making ill-informed comparisons.

Ian Michler – Blood Lions team
We would suggest that a study be done showing the employment count per square kilometre for each agricultural sector and the predator breeding industry. It is our assessment that breeding lions requires fewer workers than planting and harvesting maize and many jobs are being lost to the voluntourism sector.

Fiona Miles – Director, Four Paws South Africa
We agree with the DEA that rural employment and migration [to] cities is an extremely complex phenomenon that cannot be linked exclusively to the canned lion industry.

However, what cannot be disputed is that the canned lion industry and the shifting of land to this practice has certainly not assisted in reversing this phenomenon in any way. The industry creates very little employment compared to other agricultural activities as even running a traditional safari destination and eco-tourism would result in more gainful employment than a canned hunting operation.

Farms that traditionally would be run as safari destinations have been converted into breeding facilities or simply venues for the hunt. The lion is released onto that land shortly before the arrival of the hunter. The hunter is taken to the land and shoots his lion to then just leave again. That land is not being utilised in any constructive manner that will cause employment.

8. There have been IUCN studies proving that hunting is a wasteful use of land. Are you aware of these studies and if so why does the DEA appear to be ignoring them?

[DEA's response]
DEA is aware of IUCN studies that found the opposite; in fact, the IUCN SSC Sustainable Use and Livelihoods Specialist Group has published a number of documents that the DEA found extremely useful. The author is encouraged to engage with the Specialist Group on their work.

Fiona Miles — Director, Four Paws South Africa
The question here should be centred around what kind of hunting is occurring on that land. As mentioned previously, traditional hunting safaris in areas where the animals are largely left to live 'normal' lives are far more useful than canned lion hunting [where] the land is underutilised.

9. Are you aware of the damage that canned hunting is doing to Brand South Africa, and the economic impact of this damage?

[DEA's response]
The DEA has taken note of statements relating to concerns about the possible impact on brand South Africa. To date no information relating to the economic damage to relevant industries, including the tourism industry has been provided to the Department.

Ian Michler — Blood Lions team
There is little doubt that canned hunting has had and is still having a detrimental effect on Brand South Africa. Why does DEA say they want proof of economic damage, when tourism authorities such as the Past Minister of Tourism, Hon. Derek Hanekom, have said (when interviewed for Blood Lions™): 'I think it has already damaged Brand South Africa — how significantly I'm not really able to tell. The practice of canned lion hunting or breeding in captivity comes with a lot of negativity and therefore it does and probably will do further reputational damage unless we take some more decisive measures to discourage it.' And more recently, Sisa Ntshona, CEO SA Tourism stated: 'It is extremely relevant and topical at the moment, and gives us an opportunity to unequivocally state our position. South African Tourism does not promote or endorse any interaction with wild animals such as the petting of wild cats, interacting with elephants and walking with lions, cheetahs and so on. http://cdn.nowmedia.co.za/NowMedia/TU/Webinar_responses_submit_TU_5Dec.pdf

Fiona Miles — Director, Four Paws South Africa

To on the one hand confirm that the DEA is aware of the negative impact and to then try and equate that to no real economic damage is simply missing the point. As a country, we cannot and should not be involved with activities that are deemed to be ethically suspect.

This is a very short-term view on a subject that will have a very long-term impact. If we lose our position as a leading conservation-driven destination (if we have not already) then it is a very slippery slope to get back up.

As a country, we are blessed with amazing natural beauty and resources and how we manage them is critical to our future survival. To turn a blind eye to the impact that canned lion hunting has on our image and standing in the world (negative economic impact or not) is setting us up for disaster.

10. Why did the South African government lobby CITES for an exemption for South African captive-bred lions from the zero quota for lion body parts?

[DEA's response]

The South African government did not lobby CITES for exemptions. As you should know, an Appendix I listing was proposed for all African Lion. South Africa did not support the proposed listing because its African lion population is not in decline. In fact, the population of African lion has just been listed as Least Concern in terms of the revised IUCN Red List. During discussions relating to the proposed listing, the range States and other CITES Parties agreed to place a zero quota on the trade in bones from wild sources for commercial purposes and to include a quota to be determined by South Africa for bone originating from captive-breeding facilities. South Africa agreed to this annotation, as a risk-averse intervention. This is considered a risk-averse intervention because of concerns relating to the shift in lion and tiger bone trade observed and recorded in a study commissioned by TRAFFIC. It was noted that when the trade in tiger bone was banned; the trade shifted and bones were sourced from South Africa, available as a by-product of the hunting of captive-bred lions. One of the main concerns is that lion bones may be illegally sourced from wild lion populations if the trade in the bones originating from captive-bred lions is prohibited. A well-regulated trade will enable the Department to monitor a number of issues relating to the trade, including the possible impact on the wild populations.

Ian Michler – Blood Lions team
To a degree, the answer is correct. But it again begs the question, why wait until we have a decline in wild populations before acting? The South African government voted at this same CITES conference to support a ban in the trade in tiger parts because of pressure on wild populations and then they go and ask for a quota to trade lion bones. It is nonsensical.

Fiona Miles – Director, Four Paws South Africa
The DEA mentions a great deal about the resolutions passed at CITES but again fails to mention the agreed need for a comprehensive study. They also fail to mention how they have determined that the African lion population is not in decline. How did they derive this conclusion? Do their figures include wild, population managed and canned lions?

We can again bring up studies that state in reality the wild African lion population is in fact declining.

Another point of concern here is 'a well-regulated trade'. We have not seen any evidence to show how this industry and trade will be regulated in practice. The DEA has suggested processes but do they have the man power and budget to enforce these effectively and also [control] the illegal trade?

If we open the door to allow some trade, it will be more likely that nefarious trade will follow shortly afterwards.

11. Many think that this exemption will open a massive loophole for trading illegally obtained bones and other body parts. Do you not accept that you may actually have helped increase poaching by creating this legal loophole, and eventually this will negatively impact Africa's few remaining wild lions?

[DEA's response]
The process to regulate the trade will address concerns relating to the entry of illegally obtained bones. The following process is proposed:
- The quota will be managed at a national level
- International trade will be restricted to trade in skeletons only (not individual pieces, bone pieces, etc)
- Upon receipt of an application from a captive-breeding operation (CBO)/hunting farm, the province will confirm with DEA whether a quota is available

- The province will evaluate the application and determine whether the relevant permit can be issued
- Skeletons will be packed separately at source (CBO/hunting farm), weighed, tagged and a DNA sample will be taken
- Quota numbers will be indicated on all permits (e.g. killing/ hunting/ selling/ buying/ transporting/ exporting)
- Consignment to be inspected (and weighed) and permit endorsed at port of exit; random DNA samples will be collected.

Added to that, monitoring will be on-going and further studies as agreed by CITES Parties will also be undertaken by the CITES Secretariat.

Ian Michler — Blood Lions team

At the DEA meeting on Lion Bone Quotas 2017 on 18 January 2017, DEA stated that they needed 'to improve enforcement of current regulations on hunting of lion and monitoring of exports of bones'. They also said there was 'uncertainly about the role and impact of the lion bone trade', and listed their key challenges as being: Creating non-compliance, Marking of the captive-bred bones, Management of the quota, Compliance and Enforcement, Capacity, Sources of the bones (i.e. taxidermists, hunting farms, breeding farms, zoos, individuals, rehabilitation facilities).

Fiona Miles — Director, Four Paws South Africa

As mentioned in the previous question, does the department have the manpower and budget to enforce the proposed strategy?

12. Was your request for the exemption based on science or on the commercial requirements of your captive-lion breeders?

[DEA's response]

Please refer to responses above.

13. A figure of 800 lion carcasses for export has recently been arrived at. On what basis was this figure calculated?

(DEA's response)

It is based on an assessment done by the South African National Biodiversity Institute of previous years' trade data (10 years trade data) (including trade in bones and hunting trophies).

Ian Michler – Blood Lions team

Furthermore, at the DEA Meeting on Lion Bone Quotas on 18 January 2017, SANBI's Michelle Pfab was recorded as saying there was no actual methodology used to determine the proposed export figure of 800 lion carcasses. DEA stated that they do not currently have a non-detriment finding (NDF) for these captive-bred exports as required under CITES, although they agreed this was vitally important to study the impact of trade in captive-lion parts on wild populations. So, why has this not yet been commissioned?

Fiona Miles – Director, Four Paws South Africa

We refer to above-mentioned and the agreement at CITES that a comprehensive study is required.

As part of several concerned environmental organisations we have not been able to get the DEA to provide any evidence or scientific data of how they came to this figure. They seem to be unable to truly justify how they derived this figure.

14. Is the DEA's position on captive-lion breeding and canned hunting mainly influenced by political interests, commercial interests, or science-based information?

(DEA's response)

It should be noted that the Department fulfils a policy formulation and regulatory function based on its mandate, which is derived from the Constitution of the Republic of South Africa, and more specifically Section 24 of the Constitution. Decisions relating to any aspect involving the environment (including biodiversity) are based on the Constitution and the legal mandate given to the Minister by Parliament. The National Environmental Management: Biodiversity Act, 2004 (Act No 10 of 2004), a legislation passed by the Parliament of the Republic of South Africa, provides the Minister of Environmental Affairs with a legal mandate on biodiversity and conservation matters in the country.

Ian Michler – Blood Lions team

The government's answer is a long-winded way of saying that the term 'sustainable use' appears in the Constitution and, because of this, they are entitled to use wildlife for whatever commercial purposes they wish. Currently, thinking and policies that sanction the use and abuse of wildlife dominate in South African wildlife management circles.

Fiona Miles – Director, Four Paws South Africa

It is our belief that an organisation such as DEA should always put the welfare and management of our natural resources first. Political and commercial interest should be secondary. It is, however, not for us as an organisation to try and postulate what the reasoning is behind why the DEA does what it does. Ours is rather to input into the debate and ensure that we always place the animals and their welfare first.

ALBI MODISE
CHIEF DIRECTOR: COMMUNICATIONS
DEPARTMENT OF ENVIRONMENTAL AFFAIRS

Gareth Patterson commented as follows:

'DEA's reply to the questions is indicative (along with the current proposals to export lion bones, to reopen trade in rhino horn, to lift the moratorium on leopard trophy hunting, and seemingly having no inclination to phase out the lion breeding/canned lion industry) that the Department is still embracing the pro-use, pro-trophy hunting and pro-wildlife trading utilitarian conservation doctrine that existed in South Africa prior to our first democratic elections in 1994. This outdated utilitarian conservation doctrine is rooted in the colonial past.

As a maturing African democracy, we now have the opportunity of proudly re-embracing and implementing an Afrocentric rooted culture of environmentalism which existed in our continent prior to colonisation. The demand for ivory, rhino horn, hardwood trees, lion bones, and the western culture of killing lions and other species purely for so-called 'sport' (trophy hunting), these are not African demands, but demands of those from outside Africa. With a renaissance of African Environmentalism we could lessen the damage of these detrimental demands on our wildlife and our wild places.

I invite your readers to learn more about African Environmentalism by visiting the website of the Sekai African Environmentalism Group.'

Chris Mercer from the Campaign Against Canned Hunting had the following opinions on the DEA's answers:

'Generally the answers taken together – because of course the questions are all related to each other – show a most singular wilful diligence in ignorance. Any questions which suggest that the lion farms should be closed down and the lion-bone trade banned are met with the stock response 'no scientific proof of harm'.

Per contra, when it comes to promoting the lion-bone trade, the DEA is eager to overlook the lack of any scientific proof, and rush to decide that lion bones should be exported in numbers based upon the previous year's trade figures.

The combined weight of 16,000 leading world conservation scientists is glibly dismissed as a mere right to free speech. Just someone else's opinion.

There is no attempt to understand why all the leading scientists urged the SA government to phase out lion farming.

What these answers prove to me beyond any doubt is that SA conservation structures have been captured by the hunting industry, and my conviction is reinforced by the exclusion of the media when the DEA holds its secret meetings at remote locations with hunting industry representatives, including Safari Club International from the USA.'

Campaign Against Canned Hunting

Chris Mercer, founder of CACH and tireless campaigner

ACRONYMS

- CACH   Campaign Against Canned Hunting
- CITES   Convention on International Trade in Endangered Species
- CMS   Convention on Migratory Species
- CPHCSA   The Custodians of Professional Hunting and Conservation South Africa
- DEA   Department of Environmental Affairs
- DLP   Drakenstein Lion Park
- HR   Human Resources
- HWC   Human-Wildlife Conflict
- IFAW   International Fund for Animal Welfare
- IUCN   International Union for Conservation of Nature
- NAPHA   Namibia Professional Hunters' Association
- OPHAA   The Operators and Professional Hunters' Associations of Africa
- PHASA   Professional Hunters' Association of South Africa
- PH   Professional hunter
- SANBI   South African National Biodiversity Institute
- SAPA   South African Predator Association
- SCI   Safari Club International
- TRAFFIC   Trade Records Analysis of Flora and Fauna in Commerce

The IUCN Red List indicates lion populations declined by 43% between 1993 and 2014.

APPENDIX 3

USEFUL WEBSITES

- Africa Wildlife Foundation – www.awf.org
- Big-cat Rescue – www.bigcatrescue.org
- Blood Lions – www.bloodlions.org
- Born Free Foundation – www.bornfree.org.uk
- Campaign Against Canned Hunting – www.cannedlion.org
- CITES – www.cites.org
- Drakenstein Lion Park – lionrescue.org.za
- Ewaso Lions – www.ewasolions.org
- Four Paws – www.four-paws.org.uk
- IFAW – www.ifaw.org
- Let Lions Live – www.letlionslive.org
- LionAid – https://lionaid.org
- Namibia Professional Hunters' Association – www.napha-namibia.com
- Operators and Professional Hunters' Associations of Africa – https://ophaa.org
- Panthera Africa – pantheraafrica.com
- Professional Hunters' Association of South Africa (PHASA) – www.phasa.co.za
- Richard Peirce – www.peirceshark.com
- Sekai African Environmentalism Group – www.sekaiafrica.com
- South African Predator Association (SAPA) – www.sapredators.co.za
- WWF Help Lions – www.wwf.org.uk/lions

A sign directs visitors to the pub at the Moreson ranch near Vrede.